VISIONS
OF EUROPE

Richard Kearney
– RTE Series

April 18, 97

for Helen,

with best wishes,

Richard

Also by Richard Kearney from Wolfhound Press

TRANSITIONS: NARRATIVES IN MODERN IRISH CULTURE
(Wolfhound Press 1987; Manchester University Press, 1988)
THE IRISH MIND: EXPLORING INTELLECTUAL TRADITIONS
(Wolfhound Press and Humanities Press, New Jersey, 1985)
THE CRANE BAG BOOK OF IRISH STUDIES, VOLUME II (1982–1985)
(Wolfhound Press, 1987)
ACROSS THE FRONTIERS: IRELAND IN THE 1990S
(Wolfhound Press, 1988)
MIGRATIONS: THE IRISH AT HOME AND ABROAD
(Wolfhound Press, 1989)

Other titles by Richard Kearney

POÉTIQUE DU POSSIBLE (Beauchesne, Paris, 1984)
MYTH AND MOTHERLAND (Field Day Publications, 1984)
DIALOGUES WITH CONTEMPORARY CONTINENTAL THINKERS
(Manchester University Press, 1984)
MODERN MOVEMENTS IN EUROPEAN PHILOSOPHY
(Manchester University Press, 1986; St Martin's Press, New York)
THE WAKE OF IMAGINATION
(Hutchinson and Routledge, London, 1988;
University of Minnesota Press, Minneapolis, 1989)
POETICS OF IMAGINING (HarperCollins and Routledge, 1991)
ANGEL OF PATRICK'S HILL (Raven Arts Press, 1991)
POETICS OF MODERNITY (Humanities Press, New Jersey, 1992)
HEIDEGGER ET LA QUESTION DE DIEU (Grasset, Paris, 1981)
THE CRANE BAG BOOK OF IRISH STUDIES, VOLUME I
(Blackwater Press and Colin Smythe, 1982)
LES MÉTAMORPHOSES DE LA RAISON HERMÉNEUTIQUE: PAUL RICOEUR
(Editions du Cerf, Paris, 1991)

VISIONS
OF EUROPE

Conversations on the Legacy
and Future of Europe

RICHARD KEARNEY
Based on the RTE Series

WOLFHOUND PRESS

First published 1992 by
WOLFHOUND PRESS
68 Mountjoy Square
Dublin 1

British Library Cataloguing in Publication Data
Visions of Europe
  I. Kearney, Richard
  940.55

  ISBN 0-86327-350-5

Cover design: Jan de Fouw
Cover photographs: RTE
Typesetting: Wolfhound Press
Printed by the Guernsey Press Co Ltd, Guernsey, Channel Isles

CONTENTS

RICHARD KEARNEY is Associate Professor of Philosophy at University College Dublin and author of many books on European thought and culture. He has lectured widely in universities in Europe and North America and has considerable experience as a broadcaster with Irish, British and French television and radio. He is a member of the Arts Council and the Higher Education Authority, and chairperson of the Irish Film Centre in Dublin.

RICHARD KEARNEY

Introduction:
Rethinking a Continent

Most talk about the New Europe has been about politics and economics. But there is another question often ignored in this debate — one that goes to the very heart and mind of Europe. I refer to the cultural question of Europe's vision of itself and of its formative relationship to the wider world beyond its historic frontiers. What images does Europe have of itself and of others? This series of dialogues explores a variety of such images with leading thinkers and writers, and challenges head-on some established assumptions about what it means to be European.

Many of us think of Europe as a geographical continent of old frontiers and flags. In recent times, we have been obliged to think again. Western Europe has experienced the emergence of an economic space resounding with talk of common trade and tariffs, while to the East we have witnessed an unfolding drama of rapidly shifting borders. Berlin, Budapest, Bucharest, Belgrade — the very mention of these names recalls how decisive the changes have been. The multi-coloured map we gazed upon at school no longer tells the full story. Traditional borders have become both too large and too small: too large to cater for the growing sense of regional differences in Europe, and too small to respond to the movement towards European integration. We are speaking of a continent in metamorphosis.

This whole debate raises fundamental questions about the very nature of sovereignty, about the meaning of words like nationalism and federalism, about the need to balance the moves to European unity with a greater recognition of cultural and linguistic diversity (see Ascherson and Taylor in particular). No one can deny that a battle of ideas is being waged at present over the very soul of Europe; and that the outcome of this battle will determine the future contours of this continent.

One of the most telling revisions of the European landscape in recent years has been the re-emergence of a 'middle' Europe between the historical poles of East and West. This signals the return of an eclipsed part of the European body and releases voices silenced during almost fifty years of Cold War. One such voice is Marin Sorescu, a Romanian poet and painter, suppressed under the Ceaucescu regime and from whose house in Bucharest the recent revolution in Romania was launched. In our introductory programme to the series he had these words to say:

> 'When the people went out onto the streets they became both citizens and poets. Because the revolution was a true revolution, every citizen became a poet. It was like a moment of inspiration, with the same word on everybody's lips — "liberty". At that moment, artists like Dinescu and Karamitru played a key role: with shooting everywhere and confusion they became public figures who spoke for and with the people — even declaring the revolution on national television. And we also took great courage from the role played by our fellow poet, Václav Havel, in the Czech revolution. Now that the revolution is over, however, poets are not keen to take up power; we know from history that poets who become involved in politics for too long lose their talent, they make mistakes — both as poets and politicians'.

Several of the dialogues which follow (and especially those with other 'middle Europeans' such as Havel, Holub and Kristeva) return to this crucial relationship between intellectuals and power, between writers and their emerging society.

The various contributors to this series come from very different countries and cultures. Some still remember the last war and the terrible crimes of Hitler, Mussolini and Stalin committed in the name of a European Empire. Others stress the positive achievements of art, science and law which have made European modernity a password throughout the globe (see Heaney,

Steiner, Voinovich, Robinson). But however various their verdicts, all speak as independent minds. They are public figures unbound by partisan policy. They are, all of them, people who function in the open realm of ideas and images, of education and the media, without constraints of party or propaganda. The purpose of these dialogues is to allow each of these migrant minds to speak of Europe in alternative ways, in a manner more personal and unpredictable than in normal current affairs commentary.

All of my interlocutors share a desire to tell the story of Europe. This means retelling its history in their own particular way and responding to others' views. Above all, as Paul Ricoeur puts it, it means an 'exchange of memories'. For it is only by remembering each other's past, by sharing each other's sufferings and aspirations, that we begin to reinvent a future of mutual respect and atonement.

But can Europe reinvent itself?

Can it discriminate between its different legacies — the good, the bad and the ugly?

Can it contribute to a new concept of universality freed from the legacy of world domination (known today as Euro-centrism)?

Can we construct a unity which also respects diversity and difference?

Can we work towards new models of international community in the face of the recent collapse of trans-national states like Yugoslavia and the Soviet Union?

Can the project of a United Europe avoid the pitfalls of a Fortress Europe by keeping itself open to its 'others' — not only the other nations outside the twelve member states of the EC but also its non-European neighbours to the East and South?

More pressingly, is it possible for Europe to survive the current crisis of collective identity epitomised by the erosion of the old ideologies, and resulting in a general turning inwards — at times, indeed, in the excesses of compulsive nationalism and racism?

These are some of the questions which recur throughout these exchanges. Several of the contributors — Said and Warner in particular — recall Europe's debts and responsibilities to the other continents. Indeed, we are reminded that the very name of Europe is itself derived from a tradition lying somewhere between Africa and the Middle East! As legend has it, *Europa* was carried by her father across the Mediterranean to Greece but never abandoned her non-European origins.

Such reminders open a Pandora's box of further questions. Would the universalist culture of Athens ever have emerged without its crucial borrowings from Babylonia and Egypt? Can we ignore the fact that the European tradition of Judaeo-Christianity first arose in the lands of the Middle East? Would the teachings of Aristotle and Greek philosophy ever have returned to the heart of Europe after the dark ages if it wasn't for the work of great Arab thinkers like Avicenna and Averroes? And is it not the case that seminal cultures like Byzantium and Andalusia were themselves melting pots of hybrid cultures and creeds? Finally, we may ask if Europe's self-recollection today should not include both a repossession of its rich cultural heritage *and* a recognition of the sins committed in its name — from colonial domination to ecological waste?

The interviews which follow, based on edited versions of the original RTE series, seek to initiate a dialectic between different and sometimes conflicting views. No attempt by the European family to define itself can succeed unless it also remains answerable to its 'others' — those non-European communities which have historically contributed, and continue to contribute, to its identity and development. The concept of the 'one' — a founding principle of European civilisation inherited from the Greek and Judaeo-Christian traditions — already includes the 'stranger' as part of its self-understanding. The European gift of universality is — as Darras and Eco make plain — one which must accommodate cultural pluralism and polyphony if it is to be true to its promises. The alternative is uniformity and intolerance.

What are the implications of such thinking for a New Europe? Whatever form political and economic integration takes in the years to come, it is almost certain to go beyond the old model of centralised Nation States. The newly emerging Europe, as various contributors below suggest, has a unique opportunity to be truly democratic by fostering notions of sovereignty that are inclusive rather than absolute, shared rather than insular, disseminated rather than closed in upon some bureaucratic centre. This would involve not only a greater devolution of powers to smaller regions within the European Nation States, but also a greater awareness of Europe's debts and duties to the planet as a whole.

Europe is like Janus. It has a good face and a bad face. The bad grows from its sometimes arrogant attempt to shape the world in its own image. The good comes from its readiness, once again on probation at this decisive moment in history, to shape itself in the image of a wider world.

I wish to thank all those who contributed to the production of these dialogues, in particular Michael Garvey, series producer at RTE; Raymond Georis and Miriam Hederman of the European Cultural Foundation; Andrew Carpenter, Kevin Barry and Augustine Martin of University College Dublin and the Baileys Lecture series; Laurence Cassidy and the Board of the Dublin International Writers' Conference, 1991.

NEAL ASCHERSON is a British author and journalist. He has written as political correspondent for the *Scotsman* and as European correspondent for the *Independent on Sunday*. His most recent book is *Games with Shadows*.

NEAL ASCHERSON

Nations and Regions

Richard Kearney: *Do you believe the European Enlightenment made a positive contribution to modernity?*

Neal Ascherson: I think what it gained above all was the sense of citizenship and a sense of universality. The Enlightenment said two things. First of all, it said that people have rights. Secondly, it said all solutions, all ideals, apply equally to everybody. Liberty, equality, fraternity — these are the birth rights of all human beings all over the earth, not just in Europe, and all are equally entitled to them. So there is a universalism of value. Now, out of that, you can go in two different ways. On the one hand you got in Europe the view that certain ideologies were totally true and that since their values were universal, they should be imposed on everybody; this led straight to totalitarian systems, to dictatorship. The other stream from the Enlightenment is a continuous series of empowerings or disseminations of power, of constantly discovering ways in which people at the bottom of the social heap, or undiscovered populations in remote places, can be brought into the light of culture, education and of making their innate rights — as they were known in those good old days — a reality by showing them how to use them and creating conditions in which they could use them.

Isn't there a third path leading from the declaration of those rights of liberty, fraternity and equality? I'm thinking of the way in which Napoleon interpreted that universalism of citizen rights to be the rights of Frenchmen — and turned the universalism of the French revolution into imperialism by invading other countries and 'liberating' them into a new French Empire ...

Yes, there has been that, and I think it was rather characteristic of the results of the Enlightenment. But then again, Germany is very similar. Germany eventually got into this strange intellectual position in which it said the expansion of Germany is actually a great move forward because Germany is so advanced that it is no longer just a Nation State, it actually *is* universality itself. We are the first bit of the future that exists, and if we roll over other bits of Europe they will have the immense privilege of living under the boots of our Grenadiers and the tracks of our tanks, of joining the future and leaving behind their petty, divisive particularity. This was a kind of justification for monstrous imperialism.

But you would see both the Napoleonic and Hitlerite projects as a perversion of universalism.

Yes, it is a perversion. But it goes back further. There is a difficulty here in that the Enlightenment is a creed for intellectuals. Intellectuals build systems: systems on the whole do not allow for exceptions. They lay down laws, which are supposed to apply to everybody because they correspond to the universal laws of what goes on inside all human beings, who are in many ways exactly the same. So, there is this mechanistic element which leads back to the equivalent of the mad professor in the white coat, who in this century in Europe has been the intellectual with his moustache and cup of thick black coffee and his endless newspaper, sitting at some central European café table, scribbling manifestos and going in and out of concentration camps.

Could I usher you even a little more eastwards towards central Europe? There is a lot said and written today about middle Europe — Mittel Europa — as the cradle of modern civilisation; and we have what is now almost a cult of the central European intellectual. Are you convinced by that?

Well, there is no question but that central Europe, Hapsburg Europe, developed an incredible concentration of talent, most but not all of it Jewish. After the fall of the Hapsburg empire, of course, most of it had to leave or was annihilated. Many of the Jewish intellectuals fled abroad where most of their influence on the human race was effected. There is a great sentimentalism about central Europe which says that if only we could have the old Hapsburg empire back, we could all rejoin each other, we could sink these nation states back into a regional association.

So, it sort of sounds nice and it is a pretty picture; but one should never forget the other side. Central Europe wasn't just a place of sentimental ideas, of progressive scientific research. It was also the place where the most terrible of these distortions of the Enlightenment arose. Central European intellectuals first of all invented romantic nationalism, which, as I think, has a good side and a bad side; but then they invented totalitarianism in that part of the world. That's where these ideas first came from. This is where Marxism, but particularly the perversions of Marxism, originated. This is where Fascism essentially arose — in this part of Europe, middle Europe, with its hatreds, its confusions, its whirling melting-pot of populations, in social change, national change, hating each other, looking for ways out, dreaming of somebody else to punish.

I think few people would quarrel with the cultural advantages of regional or national expression, but many would say it lacks, and will always lack, any kind of real political clout. The European Community in Brussels and Strasbourg has recently introduced the notion of subsidiarity to counter that particular accusation. Do you think that this is a persuasive principle?

I think we have to explain what subsidiarity means. It is an appalling word, describing something very attractive and quite simple. What it means is that nothing should be done at a higher level which can be done at a lower level. The basic unit of human beings is the local community. If they want to establish another body, let's say a district council, above themselves, to take on some of the things which they can't do, they have the right to do that. And if the district councils want to associate and establish regional councils, and these, in turn, a national government, they can do that. But where it all starts is *at the bottom*, with what many people in Europe call the commune or *communa* — there are many different words for it; but this is the basic unit and this is where sovereignty really starts.

The res publica?

That's right. You could put it like that. The basic unit is communal self-government.

Local participatory democracy?

It is. Of course, it can be more democratic or less democratic in this or that particular cell of democracy. But the point is, the power goes upwards from that.

Again, it sounds lovely, but is that principle practicable, and is it at work in Europe as we speak now?
It is at work in many countries as we speak. Most spectacularly it is at work in Germany.

In the Länder system, you mean?
Yes. In western Germany it works extremely well. People are very relaxed with it, they're very happy with it, and it forms a sort of background to people's approach to politics, and morality, and social life.

And how does it work? How much power does each Länd or region have within the new united Germany?
Well, in a way, you see, you're already begging the question. The point is, how much does the basic cell have? And the answer is, quite a lot. And they delegate upwards.

In what ways? Can they levy taxes?
Yes, they often do. The *Gemeinde*, which is a kind of small market town, and the area around it can levy something. So, yes. And then, a *Länd*, which is a state of the federation, can have several million people as a population ...

Bavaria would be such a Länd ...
Bavaria would be one, for example.

And North Rhine Westphalia another.
That's an interesting point, because that shows you different sorts of region. You have some regions which are essentially the remains of what was once a self-governing kingdom, like Bavaria. And you have others which were set up for political reasons like North Rhine Westphalia, created by the Allies after the war.

And yet it has been a spectacular success.
It was the part of Germany which contained the Ruhr, the main industrial basin of western Germany, which was reconstructed

and then decayed, as all those industries decayed in the Sixties and Seventies. But it has this great North Rhine Westphalian loyalty, a sort of patriotism. It works extremely well.

There are some who would say, including Margaret Thatcher in her day, that we are heading towards a Euro-Empire, where the old and cherished notions of national independence, sovereignty and identity, are going to be subverted. Do you subscribe to that view?

I subscribe only to half of it. I think that if one argues that national sovereignty is being transmuted by the new Europe, and changed into something else and eaten away, then I would agree with it. But national identity is not. It depends on what you mean by 'national', after all. What is going to come about is not, I think, a super Empire. There are certain trends obviously in the community, pointing towards an enormous irresponsible bureaucracy. But it's not going to happen, because the other institutions of the community, and the nature of the countries themselves, won't allow it.

And how do you see it developing?

I see this United Europe as a place which, like a sort of organism, is going to form an outer skin around itself. And within that outer skin, the present kind of skins which separate one Nation State from another will suddenly become porous and they'll cease to matter. They are already becoming porous. National boundaries, national State frontiers are already fading away. The existing Nation State is losing power, but power drains away in two directions — upwards to Brussels, or Strasbourg, or wherever it may be, but downwards also. And that downwards movement is what really interests me, because it's going downwards to sub-nations and smaller units.

But how do we know that's not just a utopian wish, mere rhetoric emanating from Brussels as a sop to the poorer underdeveloped regions by way of saying, 'if you go for a United Europe, we'll give you some kind of power as compensation'?

I think the answer to that is connected with the way in which the concept of region has changed so much.

Because it was traditionally associated with something backward, and reactionary, and rural.

Yes, it had two kinds of negative connotation. It had, first of all, the connotation of province — it's a province, it's dark, it's superstitious, it's backward, no doubt it's terribly poor as well, and it has a kind of primitive grievance which somebody will have to deal with. And then came the economic definition of regionalism as something negative. This was especially so in British thinking. The region was the place of economic disaster, the rust-belt, the distant north where everything fell to bits and there was mass unemployment and you had to have regional assistance. A region was a disaster area.

So when did this change?

It began to change around the 1970s. For about the first twenty years of the Community's existence there was only one State which was based on the regional structure, which was a member of it — and that was West Germany which was a federation. But then things started to change, and one state after another began to break up its old centralised character, in different degrees. Italy has now got fifteen regions. France has twenty-two regions since the early Eighties. It was a very surprising change. But this was not only happening in France, traditionally a centralised Nation State. Spain is another obvious example. After the fall of Franco, the 1978 Constitution decentralised Spain and allowed regions to take an immense amount of autonomy to themselves — the Basque region is one case, Catalonia another, and there are many others — Galicia and Andalusia, and so on.

And what about Belgium? Could you argue that Belgium is quasi-federal?

Yes, you could. The present solution to the eternal Belgian problems, if it is a solution, is really federal. Belgium now effectively consists of three parts — Flanders, the Walloon section, and Brussels itself.

Why then are Britain and Ireland the two most centralised Nation States in the European Community today? What could we gain from looking at our neighbours on the Continent?

I'd be cautious about saying why the plague of centralism affects Ireland, but I suspect it is something inherited unconsciously from the old British State. And Britain is something I can talk about. Britain is a very, very archaic State form. There is nothing else like it in Europe. Indeed, there is very little like it in the developed world at all, because the system is one of *absolute sovereignty*. What happened in the seventeenth century was that the English parliament just took absolutism away from the kings, from the divine right of kings, and gave it to parliament, where it still is. So there is no concept of *popular sovereignty*. Instead, you have an elected parliament, but it is completely sovereign — it is not subject to the people as a concept, it is not subject to a constitution. Now, what this means, for our purposes, is that the British parliament cannot give away power. It *can* give it away forever, completely, but what it cannot do is federate, effectively regionalise or devolve, because at any moment it retains the right to take it back — thereby making federation impossible.

And are not the inhabitants of Great Britain, at least in principle, subjects rather than citizens? Does that terminological difference actually mean something?

I think it does. A *citizen* is somebody who had a status in constitutional law: he is a member of the people and sovereignty starts at the bottom with the people, leading up towards the apex of the pyramid. Power does not flow down. In the British State to this day, power flows from the apex of the pyramid, symbolised by the monarch, downward, like a sort of shower of gold, or trickle of influence, into the population. In constitutional law, the flow of power is the other way around. Somebody who lives in a State where power comes down from the top is a *subject*. Somebody who lives in a country with popular sovereignty, where power goes up from the people towards its representatives at the top, is a citizen. And a citizen has rights, prescriptive rights, which can be found in the constitution.

Isn't there something almost contradictory then in the notion of a British Nation State being centralised, with absolute sovereignty running from the top to the bottom, and yet being in effect a Nation State made up of different nations — Northern Ireland, Scotland, Wales and England itself?

I think this is why the real challenge to the nature of the British State, which is going on at the moment — and it is — is a spreading idea even in England. The British State is a multinational State which in a way refuses to admit it. At the moment it consists of England, Northern Ireland, Scotland and Wales, and yet the sovereignty of Parliament, an English-dominated parliament, over those parts, is almost total. There is very little room for manoeuvre. In order to approach regionalism of some kind, which would fit into the currently growing European concept of a *Europe of the regions*, the way forward has got to be a change in the very basic constitutional doctrine of the British State. They've got to admit, first of all, that this is a multinational State; secondly, that power which is devolved or federated away to the component nations of this State cannot simply be taken back; and thirdly, they've got to break this age-old tradition of increasingly centralising authority. One of the awful things, to me at least, about the Thatcher period was that you had this rhetoric about smaller and smaller government, government withdrawing from economic management and leaving society to manage itself. But the practice was a *continuous* draining of State power to the centre, bleeding local authority power white, extraordinary events like the removal of the elected Authority for London itself, which for many years now has had no elected Authority at all.

And the Scots have been very active too in saying no to that process. You're a Scotsman and, as you know, the Scottish Nationalist Party and the Scottish Labour Party have been very active in arguing for a solution to the Scottish national problem in terms of a Europe of regions. What's the thinking behind that?

The situation in Scotland is very interesting, because essentially this is a national question. Approximately 85% of Scots want some form of Scottish parliament, either within the United Kingdom or in conditions of complete independence. I think there are several reasons why Europe has entered the Scottish debate. One is that a country like Scotland is much more directly involved with the European Community than England is through things like fisheries and agriculture. It's much more a daily matter of concern in the newspapers. But the other reason is that Europe is somehow a way of Scotland getting into the world — because, I suppose, the real urge behind the Scottish Home Rule movement, or movements, is a wish to join the world, not to leave it. Not to have everything mediated through London, but to go directly to the source of power and be represented there. The difficulty about the British system means that if the Scots wish to be at Brussels, and to be represented there, and to have their identity established at Brussels and speak directly, the rules, both of the British State and unfortunately those of the European Community to date, mean that they have to be a Nation State. So, in a curious way, Scottish nationalism, in a narrow sense of wanting to be completely independent and sovereign, has been greatly strengthened by the structure both of the Community and of Britain itself.

And yet the catchcry of the Scottish Nationalist Party is 'Independence Within Europe'. Therefore it's not an absolute independence. It is an independence that is interdependent, as it were, with other regions or regional nations.

Well, you're looking at the Scottish Nationalists, the SNP specifically, at a very tricky moment in their evolution. There *are* some people who see the road to Europe as leading to Scottish independence. That is all they care about. There are others who say, we want to be part of Europe and we want our society to grow up and meet the world again and we think that within Europe we can perhaps be a sort of region, but we must enter it as a Nation State and then surrender, or pool, a great deal of our power and sovereignty — our newly-won sovereignty. This is very interesting, because it is one of several different kinds of track towards a *Europe of the regions*. And there are a few nations, submerged nations, who feel that in order to become a region of this new United Europe, they have to pass through the phase of being a Nation State *first* so that they can then enter Europe and pool their sovereignty on their own terms.

A final question. At a recent conference in Belfast organised by the Cultural Traditions group, you spoke about the notion of 'home', and the importance of regional and national identity in relation to home, requiring a redefinition of home as something hospitable and open and inclusive. Could you say something about that?

Yes. That comes back to the point about nationalism, regionalism and xenophobia. The greatest luxury of making your own
home in the way that you want it is the ability to offer hospitality.
Everybody knows that. Nothing is more delightful than feeling
that you have entered the world, and you can open your doors
so that people can come. I have watched this in a lot of countries
which have made it to some form of Home Rule, self-government
or independence. I have seen the unalloyed delight of being able
to do that, to strangers, even to people whom you hated the day
before yesterday, those you despised, knew little about, to your
traditional enemies. So, I hope for that. I liked intensely what
Mary Robinson said about the Fifth Province, and about the
ideal of hospitality and opening doors to strangers, and this is
very much part of the new hope for Europe. I once went looking
for somewhere to live in Bad Gotensburg, in Germany, many
years ago. I came to this sinister, exaggerated villa which was
called Haus Stachenburg, and I went in and there was this
formidable landlady advancing towards me with a grey bun, and
a sinister expression. And behind her was an inscription in
poker-work which read — *'Mein Haus ist meine 'Welt, immer 'raus
wem's nicht gefällt'* — which means, 'My house is my world: if
you don't like it, be off with you!' That strikes me as exactly the
old narrow, exclusivist, hate-defined nationalism from which we
are now moving away.

Jacques Darras

Bankers and Poets:
Geniuses of the North

Richard Kearney: *With what particular moment would you identify the birth of modern Europe?*
Jacques Darras: With the time of the bankers, the time of the traders, people risking themselves with their currency, their coins. They came from Lombardy, from northern Italy, crossing the Alps, being protected by guards and reaching the first stage, Lyons, the central city, what we call in French *La plaque tournante* of all the conquests of Europe by the Italians. And then, travelling north, avoiding Paris, going to places like Reims and Troyes and ending up in that city of all cities, which is very dear to my own name, to my own feelings — Arras in Northern France — where the greatest fair of them all was at the time. But traders, because of their mobility, because of the mobility that is in money itself, in the exchange of goods, took along with them an exchange of ideas. You can't dissociate an exchange of goods from an exchange of ideas. I think that Europe developed from that sort of trading of ideas, currencies and fashions, over the counters, in the open air of an Arras square, for instance. Poets were there too. Of course they had no money. They were begging for money all the time, from the princes, from the bankers, from the traders: being fed on a free meal here and there, and giving in exchange a poem, or cracking a joke if the banker was not charitable to them. There you had poetry, scholarship, trading and banking as well.

Today we seem to be moving towards a central European bank whose currency will be this famous ECU. We don't know what'll be on the cover of the ECU notes, but presumably it will be a variation on the round stars

JACQUES DARRAS is a French poet and Professor of Literature at the Universities of Paris and Amiens. His books include *Beyond the Tunnel of History* (1989, BBC Reith lectures), *Le génie du Nord, Conrad and the West* and *Autobiographie de l'espèce humaine.*

of Europe. And some people will feel that the old currencies where you had your king, queen, president, national hero or heroine, mattered to them in that that symbolism of money, in the figure-head on the pound note or on the coin, they had some sense of attachment, some sense that they were governing their own lives. Moving from the world of the European ECU to a broad European ecumenism (to coin a phrase) you might say we are heading towards a lowest common denominator culture: one where the shared Europe would be precisely that banal, homogenous bit we all have in common, where instead of affirming our national and regional differences, we would simply conform to the same kind of Eurospeak.

I'm no economist, but the little I know from history tells me that the ECU system was there already in the Middle Ages. I mean, you had your standard money, and what was standard money? It was gold. All the local monies, all the local currencies, operated by the gold standard. And, therefore, you could have spoken of a unification of money. Just as in the Middle Ages, Europe's gold standard, as far as language was concerned, was Latin. You could communicate with other people through Latin, as we are doing through English these days. No, I don't think the situation has changed tremendously. I'm quite sure that in the thirteenth and fourteenth centuries, people must have said, like you've just done, that there was a sense of uniformity and monotony being imposed upon them, resulting in a loss of diversity, of locality and localism. I think that's exactly what Europe is all about, trying to muster together, to bring together, throughout time, a sense of unity, while leaving chaos at the bottom. Well, this is democracy. What is democracy about, if not trying to restore, to impose, an order on top of a tremendous disorder crowding underneath?

So, would you go along with T.S. Eliot's idea that there is a whole mind of Europe which is a unity of tradition?
I think there is.

And how would you define it?
I would say it's cultural. The great price that is put on culture and scholarship has been an investment. I mean, I'm quite struck by the fact that some cities around the fourteenth century, Paris among them or the Italian cities such as Padua or Bologna, were cunning enough to understand that money as such was not

enough, that they had to invest in learning. And old cities like Arras, for instance, declined almost overnight for not understanding that it had to put its money in knowledge, science and art. There was no university created in Arras, the university was created in Paris, in La Sorbonne. And all the nations of Europe flocked to La Sorbonne.

And this investment in culture and learning was more than a cosmetic veneer?

Indeed. That's why we see the rise to prominence of northern Flemish and Dutch cities, like Antwerp, especially with the coming of printing. And that's why we witness the collapse of those old medieval cities which lacked the lucidity that might have taken them towards learning instead of just making money as bankers and traders. The lesson of modern Europe is that you cannot separate economics and culture.

Why are you so fascinated by the pan-European culture of the high Middle Ages? Again and again in your writings you come back to this, and your chosen example is often that of Burgundy. But you take various other parts of Northern Europe as well to illustrate your point. What is it about the high Middle Ages that you feel we lost, and may be recovering again?

What I feel is that there was at the time a sense of energy and dynamism in the making. The people realised that a feudal society, and feudal systems, were obsolete, on the way out, vanishing, that they were freeing themselves from that sort of order imposed upon them. They were beginning to discover the joy of freedom. This experience of freedom in Europe took place for the first time in the northern cities, not in the southern cities. And it actually happened when a few bold traders asked their freedom from the landlords, from the Church, or from the King, playing viciously and intelligently one against the other in order to acquire a real sense of liberty. A freedom for trade. Thus began a cross-frontier movement accommodating and accepting foreigners instead of levying taxes on them.

So it was a Europe of open exchange and mobility.

Absolutely. It was a Europe of free market exchange between those people of the North, and you can still see that in the layout of the cities with their famous places or squares. The French word 'place' is so beautiful in its simplicity, so open, enacting its image in Brussels for instance, or in Arras, those spaces surrounded by arcades under which the traders and the bankers sheltered themselves from the rain. You can still hear the noises of those crowds exchanging material, the clicking of the currency, and the punning of the Arras poets, who were quite numerous at the time. When I go to a place like the Place de Bruxelles, the Grand Marketplace, I can still feel that sense of openness, under the sky, with God residing where he should be, up there, not too close to Earth, leaving people, men and women to their daily considerations, their daily chores, letting them be governed by the life of the commons, the municipalities, that is, people elected from among the traders themselves.

This is a symbol for you of the birth of European democracy?
It is the birth of democracy. My contention is that actual democracy was born in the north of Europe, and this we tend to forget. We have strong misgivings about Northern culture, owing to nineteenth century cults of Germanic genius being unfortunately prolonged by Nazi history. But I think the North was once very joyous, very scholarly, open to all influences, very cosmopolitan, and this is that North that I want to recover.

This is the Netherlands, this is Flanders, this is the North of France, Burgundy ...
And Northern Italy, of course. You have that extraordinary access route that links up cities like Venice, Genoa, and Lyons, leading up to Antwerp, and even London.

But how do you account for the fact that when so many modern European Nation States — and indeed you might say European modernity — looked for precedents they could invoke as an authority, they looked to southern Europe, to Greece and Rome?
The concept of democracy may have been invented in Athens, but the actual life of democracy began in the North. I mean, French people don't want to be reminded that the name 'France' and 'French' come from the German tribe called the Franks.

Why are they so embarrassed about this?

They're embarrassed because of the successive wars, from 1870 onwards. We are supposed to be the privileged foes of the Germans; and that was unfortunately very true in the succession of bloody wars. But in France, in French, you have Franc, which is exactly the same root as freedom. I don't want to engage in some sort of pseudo-philology, but you had the sense of breaking in the very philological root, breaking free, breaking things in two or away from. French, Franc, freedom. I've come upon a very strange thing that I didn't know until quite recently, King Louis XI was the founder of our French State in the fourteenth century. That wily king played a very bad trick on my Arras compatriots at one stage, because they refused to be enlisted into the French kingdom. They looked towards Flanders, towards the Flemish people, and resisted Louis XI. He was very cunning, and started deporting the Arras people. My own name perhaps comes from the fact that my ancestors were deported at some stage and therefore called d'Arras, from Arras. The North was colonised by France. I would like my sort of decolonisation to make a smiling, historical, learning, scholarly gesture. Not a violent one at all, but giving the French a lesson in history, and reminding them of what French nationalism is based upon, what our Nation State is made of, and saying to them: 'I'd rather revert to square one, or to place one', in order to start all over again, to replace the threads that made up the tapestry, that you so absurdly broke through, or tore apart. And this is part of my fascination for the north of France, because I think that it was the laboratory of a Europe to come, that never came, that never came to pass, because instead of that we had nationalities and nationalisms. We're beginning in the new Europe to return perhaps to that tolerant and creative tapestry of the late Middle Ages. That is my hope.

If I could bring you back more specifically to the question of culture. You have argued that in the high Middle Ages we had a pan-European culture, which was decentralised into little city states or cultures which celebrated multiplicity, complexity, and produced works by painters like Bosch and Breugel who united high culture with popular culture. Was there a sense, at that time, that culture was available to the masses, to the people at large?

I think that the painters, especially the Flemish painters, meant the paintings to be contemplated and to be seen by everybody. In the churches, of course, mainly. This is true as well as far as music was concerned; the main music of the times was polyphony, which, to me, is the realisation of democracy in song. It is very austere, very cold in a way, but just listening to all those voices criss-crossing each other, and creating a volume which little by little fills up those huge naves of the cathedrals, is something I find very, very beautiful indeed. The best of European art is something which is constantly active, which has a spiritual energy about itself, which people not only try to emulate but which brings new ideas, new concepts, into today's life, into present life.

One could object that those modern artists and thinkers who tried to translate art into life often embraced some kind of reactionary politics — Céline, Pound and Heidegger ...

They are people of straw. They are the hollow men of T.S. Eliot's poem. But to take up the politics of modernism my feeling is that what we call modernism, and praise greatly because it is the *ne plus ultra* of art, serving as a forerunner of the social movements, and so on, I think that basically was a sort of reactionary movement — but in the good sense of the word. Modernism was reacting against a society that led to the First World War, that led to a general massacre of human beings, of human life. Modernism says no to that. I mean, the best modernist movement of them all took place in Zurich, the place where Joyce was at the same time as the Dada movement, where those people who happened to belong to two cultures, German and French, saw their compatriots on either side of the trenches fight themselves to death. Those very people in Zurich said no to the war. In my opinion, modernism is a saying no. Now, we can't say no forever. We've been saying no for a whole century. My feeling is that that's enough.

But writers and thinkers have a right to say no.

Of course they have a right to say no. But can we go on living on a culture of negativity? I think that we are just, perhaps, emerging out of the wasteland culture. I've never thought actually that T.S. Eliot's poem was a great masterpiece in itself, except that it gave the keynote of the century. If you don't have poets, you don't have consciences, and you don't have that sort of aim to praise the world, to praise life, to say that life is good, life is pleasurable. That's exactly what the poet says, and the poet that never says that life is pleasurable is not a poet in my eyes. There is a pleasure in the simple energy of life that a poet is there to tell us about and keep telling us about. At the same time, pleasure is so akin to suffering, is so beset by danger all around, that you have to preserve that sense of feeling alive, in touch with a greater truth, a cosmic, divine truth. That's what poets are here for and, therefore, they are very wary of political power, they dissent from political power because they say 'Your truth is not the truth'.

What sort of European culture are we entering into?

What we are entering into is very hard for me to say. What we are in need of is perhaps a new reconciliation of elite culture and popular culture, a retrieval of what is best in the Middle Ages. We are back again to that conception of the elite not dissociating itself from the people, from the population. I know it's very hard to achieve. I know it's very fashionable among the elite to have contempt for television — you still have those people in Paris who say to you, for instance, I won't let my children watch television; we have no TV set in our room. I don't agree with that at all. We have cable television, we have cable news, even if it's a zapping culture we're in, it's another type of freedom in a way. I can zap from Italian programmes to German programmes. Now, I'm not a born zapper but if I really want to apply my mind and put in the effort, for instance, to learn German, I can turn to my German news every night, and complement that by lessons in German. I think that culture for everybody is there. We are suffering from an excess, an over-abundance of culture. The problem is we need the guides, the guiding effort. People are talking of ethics, of an ethical renewal, and so on. I think that we shouldn't be taken in by those great words. Whenever somebody talks to me of ethics, I tend to become wary of it because I have the feeling that he wants to enlist me in his school, in his creed, in his camp. I think what we need are guidelines, guides, and perhaps people telling us where to apply our efforts, where best to apply our intelligence to acquire learning for ourselves. This is why the educational system is in such crisis.

Who and where are those guides?

I don't think they are yet there. They would probably be common-sense people who wouldn't despise scholarship and learning as such, who — taking the lesson from the Middle Ages — wouldn't be afraid of money, because if we really want to live in that type of society, well, it would cost a great deal. The people we want are new teachers, new minted teachers in a way. They're not in the market yet. They are to be found, they are to be turned into new preceptors, as you had for the elite during the sixteenth and seventeenth centuries taking their pupils on the *grand tour* through Italy and the continent, taking lessons on the very spot where the monuments were. We need such teachers today.

So you're advocating more democracy in education ...

Yes, a more elitist democracy.

MARINA WARNER is a novelist and
cultural historian. Her books include
*Alone of all her Sex: the myth and cult of the
Virgin Mary; Joan of Arc: the image of
female heroism; Monuments and Maidens:
the allegory of female form, The Lost Father*
and her most recent novel *Indigo*. Born of
an Italian mother and English father, she
has lived and lectured in several European
countries and was recently appointed
Tinbergen Professor at Erasmus
University, Rotterdam.

MARINA WARNER

The European Woman's Heritage

Richard Kearney: *As a writer with an Italian mother and English father who has lived much of your life in different European countries, how do you now register your particular sense of Europe?*

Marina Warner: Well, I think, in a way, you can belong to something imaginatively, which then displaces you from a particular locale. This is perhaps a helpful experience for a writer. Writing, to some extent, is connected with feeling apart, because of the writer's role of observer, or if you want to put it more rudely, as a sort of voyeur. I mean, there is a way in which you belong to something and distance yourself from it.

You mean being a part of, and apart from, at the same time?

Yes. Because I had this rather European, sort of scattered, childhood, I did feel different. I was at schools abroad, but the nature of the immediate post-War world meant I was never in an indigenous school. I was always in a foreign school in the countries where we lived.

Where, for example?

Well, I was with the French nuns in Egypt, in Cairo. And, in fact, I was with several different orders of nuns, because, at that stage, I was rather unruly. But they soon crushed my spirit, and I then became very obedient, and docile, and good, and remained in the same convent, when I finally came back to England. But when I came back, I was immediately sent to Coventry, because my English was so peculiar. I had only learnt it from grown-ups, and I also knew a bit of Arabic in those days. I also spoke a sort of Belgian French, because we'd gone to Brussels, where I had gone to another French convent. There was a distinction, or snobbish distinction, and, of course, it was not a Flemish convent. Again, this idea that the stranger comes into a place but doesn't ever fully belong to that place. And then, a woman who marries an Englishman, to some extent, loses her native identity too. And my mother was of a generation where that was possibly something that was done more; but she never lost her mother tongue, and indeed is still a teacher of Italian in England. She did offer her Italianness to my father's Englishness. She did abdicate it. We did not speak Italian at home. And we were meant to be English. She was sort of absorbed into that. But we never were successfully English, because of having lived abroad so long. I'm rather proud of it. I liked being different. I didn't mind being sent to Coventry. It made me feel special. I mean, I minded it as pain, because I was being laughed at, but I also felt special.

And this experience of cultural migration — do you see that as something positive, both for your work and for your imagination?
Yes. But I've left out one rather important thing — which is of course the one thing that my mother did not abdicate, her Catholicism. If I had been a boy, I would have been brought up a Protestant, because my father would have insisted on his line of the family continuing in the Church of England. But he felt that it was perfectly all right that my mother gave her religion to her daughters, and indeed he thought that it was a very good religion for a girl. He thought that Catholicism would particularly foster the feminine virtues. And of course this was extremely influential upon me, and has conditioned so much of the enquiry in my work.

Particularly Alone of All her Sex, *the study of the cult of the Virgin Mary.*
Yes. Mary was the most dominant, symbolic figure of my whole childhood, not just at home with my mother, who is a practising Catholic, but, of course, in the various convents. And I wanted in that book to go on a kind of personal journey to understand. I had no idea how far it would take me. I mean, one of the things about writing it was that it was exciting, that I began thinking I knew it because I had been surrounded by it, because I'd been wrapped in it, because the whole year was defined by Mary's feasts, the geography of the world consisted of visions, of places

where she'd appeared in a vision. I could have put these little flags on the map...

On the map of Europe.
Yes, on the map of Europe. Blue was the colour of my childhood. So, I thought I knew it. And then when I started work, I found that I knew nothing. That it was this extraordinary, complex history of the interaction of really every aspect of society.

So, you seem to be describing a double attitude to this theme of the Virgin Mary. On the one hand, a devotional attachment and sympathy of the heart that goes back to your Catholic childhood, and on the other hand a necessary critical detachment as a scholar who is looking historically at the development of these different stories and images and representations of Mary. But what does it tell you, as you look at that story developing, about Europe?
I think there is an inter-reaction between images of Mary and changing patterns of thought about men and women. After all, so often the definition of what is the proper function of a woman gives us an idea, by extension, of what we think about men, and how men think about themselves because very often it is they who wish women to be obedient or keep their sexuality under a certain control.

And in many respects those images were projections of a male mind or imagination.
Yes. I think the most painful, the most devastating illumination came when I realised that the enchantment of Mary, this ideal figure of beauty and grace, was actually predicated on an idea of the human as sinful, and, in particular, of the ordinary woman as peculiarly and inevitably sinful in some way in her flesh itself. So that Mary, far from being as it were the perfect path on which we were all to walk, was actually in her own *hortus conclusus*, her own enclosed garden, and the door was sealed to that. This was a way of placing the rest of us *outside* in some great untended garden, feeling as if we were in some wilderness where things were spoiled.

You were all Eves.

Yes, we were all Eves. I did rebel against that very strongly. And I have modified my views. The Church, of course, itself has gone through enormous changes since I finished the book. It was published in 1976. It's quite a while ago, and there have been many upheavals, different Popes, and also, to go back to the question of Europe, many changes in Europe which have, interestingly enough, thrown Mary again into a very important symbolic position. In Poland, for example, with Our Lady of Czestochowa. She was a national figure-head for the Solidarity movement and now, of course, has become part of this return to a kind of theocracy in which people's private lives are being ordered by the new government. I think they were even considering bannin contraception in Poland.

So, would you suggest that it's not the images of the Virgin themselves that are either good or bad, but the stories we tell about those images?

Yes. And it's the different emphases that are given. For instance in the Orthodox Church the emphasis falls differently. Its beliefs and practices are now re-entering our western Eurocentric consciousness because of greater access to eastern European countries. And they are returning to religious practice very strongly.

Bulgaria, Romania, Russia.

Yes. The Orthodox Church has rather a different history of representations of the Madonna. There is much less emphasis on virginity and the taint of the flesh. There is a married clergy which, of course, makes a huge difference to ideas about sexuality in many of the Orthodox Churches; and there is Mary's role as intercessor, which is also tremendously important in Ireland and a very merciful aspect of her persona.

Mater Misericordiae.

Yes, the Mother of Mercy, the intercessor, the mediator who stands between the wrath of God and weak humanity, interposes herself, and her milk, her Mother's milk, as it were, to turn away this just wrath. That aspect has always been very strong in the Greek and Russian Orthodox Church. They have this beautiful image of what is called the *maphorion*, which is her stole. They have it as an actual object which she holds in her hand in front of her. And this is the stole with which she covers and protects sinners.

Couldn't one argue that there's another positive side to this introduction of the Judaeo-Christian image of the Mother, which is that it introduced into a Europe of multiple cultural differences some notion of universal identification whereby people could transcend their ethnic diversities and aspire toward some common origin or goal?

I think that Incarnational thought and theology in Catholicism provides one of its most nourishing aspects because there, there's an affirmation of the human. But the difficulty has been — if we take, for example, Ireland or Italy — that the ultimate aim or purpose of woman has been defined as motherhood, maternity. There are some very shocking asides in the Church Fathers, saying things like, you know, that a man would have been a better helpmate for Adam in every way had it not been that God's purpose was procreation only, and children. There's this idea that woman is only for childbearing. And, of course, the curse in the Garden of Eden is, 'In sorrow thou shalt bring forth children'. This becomes the woman's role.

So, the transcendental aspects that you are quite rightly bringing in have rather been forgotten when it comes to Mary's motherhood. It's a highly restrictive definition of what women are for. And its cruelty is that it sets aside to some extent the life of the mind. By that I don't mean simply intellectuals. I mean the whole thinking life of a woman, which I would say — though I know this is a very difficult and problematic area — can transcend gender and sexuality. And then, it is very tough on the old, and one of the most difficult roles in history that women have lived is that of the old woman. I think that you can trace prejudices that gave rise to the great witchhunts: a whole variety of social phenomena, the numbers of old women who are homeless, prejudices about dependents, and the whole iconography of prostitution, of raddled old hags, toothless old bags. There's almost a vocabulary of derision of this sort. But a lot of this really depends on there being no place for the transcendent wisdom of women after the childbearing age. I mean, the menopause is a sort of 'curse' because it seems, in our culture, to abolish the purpose of woman. All this is very cruel, you see. It runs against the Incarnational message which should be at the centre of Christianity, which is that all of the flesh was created, God-given, and is therefore good. But it is not how, in practice, it has been borne out.

Could I bring in here two doctrinal events in the Catholic Church and the Eastern Orthodox Church, the Assumption on the one hand, and, secondly, the Greek dogma of the divinisation of the Virgin Mother? Couldn't one say that these two doctrines in a sense admit the possibility of woman achieving transcendence, being taken up into the transcendental realm from which she was traditionally excluded?

In order to express the idea that Mary had been born without original sin — conceived in the mind of God as his perfect daughter, and exempt from this stain in which all humanity was steeped — in order to represent that, interestingly enough, the Christian Churches did not resort to any of the traditional imagery of Sophia, which after all is a feminine word for wisdom in the Bible. No, they went for a late nineteenth century image of a very young, nubile girl — curiously often rather an eroticised image, nubility and innocence being intertwined as a concept of virginity. But beyond that point, beyond the dewy, rosy, bare-footed young girl who, after all, is the Madonna, the female human being enters a womanhood which cannot be identified with this pure and immaculate condition. The carnality starts at puberty, so that the Immaculate Virgin must be representative of a time before that. And, then, the Assumption. This doctrine generally holds that Mary had died but had not been corrupted, that her body had been taken to Heaven and laid at the foot of the Tree of Life in Paradise, and that it had remained there incorrupt, which is a slightly different idea than that of her not dying; but most people think that the Assumption means that Mary, rather than dying, rose heavenwards, ascended into heaven, as Jesus did in his resurrected body, that this is a sort of female resurrection. And that, of course, also overturns the idea of mortality and carnality, and there is a kind of sympathetic magic idea that the corruption of the flesh is corruption of the spirit. Again we are back into this rather barbaric Platonism by which the exterior form is a mirror of the interior form. Of course one of the other components that crushes women in the Catholic cult of purity is its connection with beauty. It is in Catholic countries like Spain where you have this extraordinary paradox between the cult of women's purity — guardianship of daughters, seclusion of women, no divorce — and the afternoon procession when men watch women and comment on their physical attributes, you know, the *passeo* in Spain, the *passeggiata* in Italy: these are Mediterranean customs, which have grown up and flourished in Catholic cultures. The sexuality of woman is her identity. It is therefore watched, assessed, praised or despised.

So the cult of the Virgin Mary is actually European in origin.

Perhaps I sound very critical, harsh, vehement. As my father used to say, 'Don't be so vehement. It's very unseemly in a woman'. But it's not so simple. I have come, now, in my forties, to wish to cut my cloth from what I have been given. I used to want to go bare-foot, you know. I used to want to strip myself of all this baggage that I'd been left as a bequest, as a Judaeo-Christian heritage. But now I want to take it up and assemble it differently. I want to have a pair of shoes, but I want to cut them differently.

To re-interpret it, to retrieve what is valuable and enabling for women, and for men, and leave aside what is not?

Yes, and I'm not alone in that. I think it is work that a lot of women writers, and indeed some men writers, are doing. And it is comparable to the work of many poets and novelists, returning to old stories and finding why they happened. An example would be Toni Morrison's *Beloved*, a very savage story about a young mother who kills a child. But by the time you've read the book, because it's set in a period just after slavery with the most extraordinary upheavals and dangers and sufferings, you really understand this terrible infanticide. The great myths and narratives are precious stores of experience and even if — as in many European myths — they affirm the order of the masculine state against female wildness, they can be retold, these stories. I mean, either to explain the past or perhaps to create a new future.

Can we understand who we are as Europeans today without retelling those stories of our foundation cultures, the Judaeo-Christian, on the one hand, which you've treated in several of your books about Western representations of women, and, on the other hand, our Graeco-Roman tradition? Is it indispensable that at least some people engage in the retelling of those stories?

Yes. There is a tension here because I think we have lost some stories, because we associate them with faith. Though the pagan gods lived on, they were set aside because they were seen to be connected with pagan religion. Again, we have a situation now in which many children don't know Bible stories, or indeed don't know the saints' lives. The Church itself has collaborated with this to some extent because in 1969 it swept away a lot of saints that I was brought up to know. Now, these stories are not told. So we have a falling-off all the time of a body of story. At the same time though, I don't want to become some kind of apostle for cultural Eurocentricity, because I do very much believe that it's dangerous to constantly harp back to the past. I abhor the kind of *revanchisme* you find it in Le Pen or other extreme nationalist and neo-fascist movements. One must stand in the present. It's a question of remembering, of having the voices behind one but keeping one's face to the times.

Isn't it curious how Le Pen marches with the Virgin Mary in one hand and Joan of Arc in the other?
Well, Le Pen's attempt to retrieve Mary or Joan of Arc for his nefarious causes is not new in France. Joan of Arc has been identified with an extreme form of patriotism since the end of the last century. Even during the Dreyfus affair, she was identified with Frenchness, as opposed to this 'adulterated' Frenchness which was Jewish Frenchness, and they attempted to use her as a figure-head for their movement. At the time, in the 1880s and 1890s, there was a much more powerful campaign to retain her for another vision of France, a more tolerant vision led particularly by the Socialist and Catholic poet, Charles Péguy, who wrote many books of beautiful verse about Joan as an emblem of a bountiful, merciful France. That's a very good example of how the symbolic can define and redefine women, and how difficult it is for the individual voice of a person who is female to emerge from the historical morass. Another example is Raphael's painting of *Parnassus* in the Vatican. He has all the assembled sages and philosophers around Apollo, and they're recognisable because we know what Dante looked like, and we know vaguely what Socrates looked like, and so forth. There's one woman, who is Sappho, but in order for the viewers of this fresco to understand that she's Sappho, she's the only person

who's labelled, because otherwise she would have been thought to be *Poesia* or *Musica* or some personification, but not an historical, individual person in history. And that is the philosophical axiom which women contend with, this sort of flight into the symbolic, this difficulty in remaining a person rather than just a persona.

You mention somewhere that one of the great legacies of European culture is the handshake. What do you mean by that?

Well, in a way, sometimes, identity resides in very small things. Instead of saying that the western world was united by the sign of the handshake, I could actually, in the modern world, have said that it's united by the suit. But I didn't say the suit. It's just that the idea of the handshake as a gesture of equality and alliance and friendship does seem to have begun in our part of the world. It was, of course, a sign of a pact, the joining of right hands, in Roman law. And it is in a way a symbol for Europe, because though it is offered in good faith, and has at times sealed pacts in good faith, it has also been tremendously betrayed.

GEORGE STEINER is internationally known for his writings on European literature, language and culture. He has held Chairs at the Universities of Cambridge and Geneva, and his books include *Real Presences, Language and Silence, After Babel, Tolstoy or Dostoevsky* and *Proofs and Three Parables*.

George Steiner

Culture — The Price you Pay

Richard Kearney: *Do you believe that there is such a thing as the 'whole mind of Europe'?*

George Steiner: I believe that there is in the history of Europe a very strong central tradition, which is by no means an easy one to live with. It is that of the Roman Empire meeting Christianity. Our Europe is still to an astonishing degree, after all the crises and changes, that Christian Roman Empire. Virgil was taken to be, rightly or wrongly, the prophet of this Empire, and Dante the great incarnation. It is very striking that when General de Gaulle, who really used to think hard about these things, was interviewed and asked: 'Are there three or four authors who are Europe to you?' he said immediately, without hesitating, 'Of course, Dante, Goethe, Chateaubriand'. The astonished interviewer, having fallen like an elephant into the pit, said, 'What, Monsieur? No Shakespeare?' And the icy smile came, 'You asked me about "Europe"'. In that joke there is a deep Roman Christian truth.

Do you believe in de Gaulle's notion, I'm thinking perhaps more culturally than politically, of a great Europe extending from the Atlantic to the Urals, as the slogan goes?

Let me answer honestly, not to make a joke, but in deep conviction: if you draw a line from Porto in western Portugal to Leningrad, but certainly *not* Moscow, you can go to something called a coffee-house, with newspapers from all over Europe, you can play chess, play dominos, you can sit all day for the price of a cup of coffee or a glass of wine, talk, read, work. Moscow, which is the beginning of Asia, has never had a coffee-house. This peculiar space — of discourse, of shared leisure, of shared exchange of disagreements — by which I mean the coffee-house, does define a very peculiar historical space roughly from western

Portugal to that line which runs south from Leningrad to Kiev and Odessa. But not east of it and not very far north.

This culture of the coffee-house you speak of would appear to be located only in certain European cities?

Yes. The shared culture we have is the culture of the *cities*. I mean, it strikes me that Europe is essentially a series, a constellation, of cities, which no other place on earth, no other civilisation, not even the United States, has ever known. When you come to think of the Moslem cities, for instance, they are all holy shrines. They are tied to religion, with the result we know at times. When you come to think of American cities, they look to me, except for a few of them, like settlements, just settled there, put on the large wide expanses, plains and so on, with no heart, with no core in them, and everybody living in the suburbs and so on, and the city just being the sky line. But when you come to Europe, what strikes you immediately is the great diversity of all the cities, each one with its historical moment of grandeur, its historical past being engraved in stone and there to be admired. And, therefore, this is our sharing, this is what we have in common. We all of us have developed and evolved from the cities, from the Italian cities and from the Flemish cities.

But couldn't one object that it is precisely the European cities that are quintessentially national — Paris as the epitome of France, London the epitome of England, Dublin the epitome of Ireland, Rome the epitome of Italy — that these are expressions of Nation States, not of some pan-European culture?

Paris is the epitome of a national city. But I would say that Paris is an exception. My theory is that France, and Paris as being representative of France, are exceptions in Europe, and the French will be a long time becoming aware of that, and they will probably have to change their ambitions and to rethink their nation, their sense of nationality, in order to adjust to the new European demands. But as soon as you mention Rome, I start smiling, because immediately I think of Venice and Milan, which are as diverse as possible, as different as possible from Rome, and which opposed themselves in the first place to Rome. What about Florence as well? What is now happening is that cities are re-emerging, as it were, over nations, taking over from nations, and entering some sort of competition, which I personally think is quite good, quite sound and healthy, because it's going to displace or tone down our national competition, which was so cruelly messy and bloody.

So what do you make of all the recent talk about a 'Europe of regions' — of the argument that, as we enter a more united Europe, some would even go as far as to say a United States of Europe, we need a counterbalancing movement of devolution and a decentralisation from the centre back to the regions? Can a unified Europe also be a Europe of differences?

Differences and diversities, yes. I love every dialect, I'm passionate. I eat languages like *hors d'oeuvres*, I just hate uniformity. In Switzerland, where I live and teach much of the year, blindfolded, you can say within ten kilometres where you are by the accent, the smell, almost the pace of the human beings you are hearing walking by you. But careful. Much of regionalism has a cruel, dark atavism. It lives by hatred: Flem against Walloon, the Basque situation, the Irish: the bombs in the pocket of the local, small, agricultural fanatical movement. Regions do tend too often to define themselves, not by remembering in joy, but in hatred. And I think we have to be very, very careful lest that come back and that flame burn again.

It seems to me that this Europe you're talking about is a Europe of high literacy, which lasted for so many hundred years, by your definition. It seems to be, in fact, a rather elitist concept of Europe: confined to the coffee houses where intellectuals talk to each other; confined to the universities; confined to the reading rooms. But one could argue that this is not something shared by the great majority of people, and indeed, that your elite notion of culture is now coming under threat. Do you see any way in which your Europe of high literacy can be preserved today?

You are quite right about the threat to this notion, and I think we could define it in very honourable terms. There is very great anger and bitterness from human beings who have felt left out, who were never elected to the club, and that anger and bitterness is increasing all around us. There is, I hope, among those of us who have been privileged, and very lucky to be in the club, some severe self-questioning: we must ask ourselves what the price for this privilege of discourse was. It did not prevent the collapse of European civilisation into ultimate barbarity: it did not prevent savagery. Instead, it may even have abetted it. We are really very, very vulnerable. And the question is, are we going to find something better than Disneyland? Twenty-eight or thirty miles from Paris, they are building a Disneyland, the second largest in the world, and they expect three hundred thousand visitors in the first few months, and it will be followed by other theme amusement parks. Apparently, Russia is now equally eager to get in on this. I look on this with despair. And yet you may ask me, do I have something better to offer? What am I going to do for human beings who don't think that reading Kant, or Joyce, or Goethe, is the be-all and the end-all of their lives, and who, nevertheless, want more leisure, want more elbow-room for sensibility? That is probably the most difficult question of all, and in a funny way, people like us, privileged intellectuals, have almost disqualified ourselves from answering it.

There is of course the opposing argument, which would hold that the electronic media of television and radio have actually made the cherished works of European culture — Shakespeare, the great operas, the great concertos — more accessible to people, because on their Saturday or Sunday nights, they now have an opportunity to tune into these classic works, and have access to them in a way that they never would have had otherwise.

This would be the optimistic point of view. It would depend on whether, having enjoyed the television programme, you might then like to buy the book, or read it to your children, or want to see the play you've liked in a living theatre. As you know better than I, this is one of the most vexed topics. Is it happening? Is there, what they call, carryover or spillover from the mass media? Some people argue that there is, without doubt, and indeed there have been classic books whose sales have rocketed after a television presentation. There is, unfortunately, a lot of evidence which goes the other way, indicating an inverse trend. The bad drives out the good gradually, and, if anything, it is the trash that is beginning to fascinate more and more. We have to guard against being both too pessimistic and too optimistic. McLuhan's idea that we knew what we were doing, doesn't seem to be quite accurate. We've out-guessed ourselves on some of it. I would not deny that certain human beings who because of distance, economics or leisure, cannot get to concert halls let alone operas, have certainly been introduced to new possibilities. But can we follow this up? Can we get these forms to them in a living mode? Unfortunately, as you know, in the British Isles, statistics show that an overwhelming number of theatres, music halls and serious film houses are closing and becoming bingo halls. If anything, television has driven out the alternative live forms.

This is what you call the 'Culture of the Secondary' — parasitism, talk about talk, images of images, rather than having access to the real presence of the work itself. But is there any sense in which that real presence can survive in anything but a mystical, or sacramental, reverence for the unique work of art, something no longer really feasible today?

Is it no longer really feasible? Let's take the really ugly end of the stick. Historians will one day say that this culture went insane when it paid one hundred million pounds for a painting; when the whole world rivalled itself in auction for one Van Gogh, one Renoir, one Picasso. And you will say, what a vulgar and mysterious way of honouring great art. Of course it is. But it comes very near to deification. Let's not forget that half the great churches of the Renaissance in Europe were built by rich patrons, trying to eclipse their neighbours — built, in fact, for conspicuous, ostentatious consumption. So there is a queer, philistine craziness about very great icons of art which continues, it's also true, in the building of new museums, of new emporia. It's not quite clear yet that, in some kind of much crueller way, the worship is gone. There is some kind of complicated idolatry. But if I could do something about it, I would like to start at the most day-to-day level. Will mothers or fathers begin to read more again to their children? Sociologists give us some evidence on that. There seems to be a deep shock, particularly in the middle class, about the fact that the child has never heard its parents' voices reading to it, reading good books to it. We're beginning, perhaps, to go back to certain possibilities. I think we're in a stage of acute conflict and transition where on both sides of the ledger you can find evidence. But the picture is not all black. The most terrifying prospect would be that of the fragile structures of privacy and of leisure being broken down by starvation, by mass migration which could come from eastern Europe, or by the breakdown of civil forms of organisation, legalism and economic exchange in some of the critical areas. If I had to choose some kind of insane dictatorship, it would be to try to bring back the little silence into our lives. The latest estimate is that about 87% of adolescents cannot read without hearing a radio, a record-player, a cassette, a long-playing disc, or television in the background. That electronic noise has become the *sine qua non*, the condition, of any act of attempted attention. If that is true, then something is happening to the old cortex which we don't fully understand.

This is what you call the 'Americanisation' of the planet, and indeed of Europe in particular, isn't it? And you do say, at one point in your recent book, Real Presences, *that the American genius is the attempt to democratise eternity and domesticate excellence. Do you think we in Europe can face that kind of competition?*

The best of America, like the best of any culture, doesn't export very well. There are very great wines which spoil when you ship them to other countries. The best of America, which has a kind of largesse of generosity, of human experimental humour and relaxation, does not export well. What does export is McDonalds, Kentucky Fried Chicken, the comic book, and all the dreadful soap operas.

So, you would say we get the worst.

We are importing the worst. We have invested our passions in the worst.

And would you support the German and French moves, particularly at a cultural level, to protect national languages and European culture from that onslaught through native film-making, native publishing and native preservation of languages?

It does not work. Walk the streets of Germany, see the presence of 'Franglais' in France, and you must recognise that the American language, as also in England, has been almost totally triumphant. With the exception of the Beatles, there has not been a major counter-statement with any kind of comparable explosive dynamic, in the English language. It's like Fairy Liquid — it comes over, it tides over, it deterges, it cleans, it purifies, it uniformises. It might go away. I see one hopeful alternative in northern Italy. There much of the best of America has been adopted — why should people not have laundromats, and proper clothes off the rack, and look better and feel better, and have decent shoes, and so on — but the double presence of Socialism and Catholicism in Italy, and the tension between them, has preserved an enormously powerful sense of national and linguistic identity. In other countries, however, we find hardly any national self-consciousness left. If it tides over, we may be in for a hundred years, two hundred years, during which human beings will say, 'Oh, shut up with all your cultural talk, we want to live decently. We actually want to have an ice box'. And for a while, that's what we're going to try — happiness is a new idea in Europe. Suppose we're on a new threshold of domestic comfort and elbow-room, in which intellectual passions are not only curiously luxurious, but positively the enemy. That's why I think we should be studying more about what is wrongly called the Dark Ages, when small groups, particularly Irish monks, scholars, wanderers, lovers of poetry and scripture and of the classics, began copying them by hand again, began founding libraries. We've been through difficult stages like this. I'm not at all pessimistic. I see a pendulum motion between a certain elitist rapture of excellence and the ordinary passion for just having a better day and night of it. One must be a sadistic, even blind, arrogant fool, ever to say to another human being, 'You have no right to live a bit better'. Of course they have that right.

So, in defence of the American ideal, one could say that it did introduce a certain egalitarian hope for many human beings, and, indeed, perhaps also a culture of tolerance for diversity, for inclusion, for what we call the melting pot.

Very much so. It has not worked all that well in America. Ethnic problems are obstinate, resistant, intractable, beyond our hopes. That very great observer, the greatest we've ever had in America, De Tocqueville, in the nineteenth century, writes that wholly prophetic sentence: 'Aristocracies create works in bronze, democracies in plaster'. This was his dictum of the American situation, to which the answer is, perhaps, 'that's the inevitable concomitant of an increase in humanity'. That is a very strong defence. My reserve is, I'm not in that business. I've given my life to teaching, to trying to say to a very small number of human beings, 'let's read Homer, and Virgil, and Dante, together.

That's what life is about'. I may be wrong, but I can't fake it. And what horrifies me about the present climate is that some of my colleagues, some of those of the intellectual profession, want it both ways. That, I think, is a piece of cant which is becoming very expensive.

Do you think in Europe we're much better? We have witnessed two World Wars this century based on the worst kinds of tribal nationalism, intolerance for the other, intolerance for diversity, which at least America has been able to accommodate with its notion of a pluralistic culture and society. Also, in recent times, we have witnessed the resurgence of an ethnic nationalism, which, some would say, augurs very badly for our immediate future. And we cannot forget, indeed, that if we are a continent and a civilisation that has produced great minds, many of those minds in our own century, such as Martin Heidegger, W.B. Yeats, Céline, proved to be very immoral people in their support for fascism. How does one answer that charge?

One cannot answer it on the factual level, it is true. But you and I have taken a kind of oath of clarity. Doctors take the Hippocratic oath — if I'm going to sign that, I'm going to behave in a certain way for the rest of my life, whatever the circumstances. We have taken an oath, which is to try to transmit excellence, to try to transmit beauty, to try to transmit form. It often seems to come a little out of the corner of Hell. That is a very central truth and enigma. But I can't fake it. A world without the figures you've mentioned, a world without the great classics, a world without the great paintings and music, would to me, if not to others, be an ash-heap. That is not to defend the Manichaean claim about the double, the blackness being a constant part of every great creation. Saints don't need to write poems. Illiterate people don't write poems, or very rarely. The cultivation of the highest powers of expression and thought does seem to go along very often with a real political inhumanity. It would be wonderful if these people were nice. They aren't. But you and I write books about them. We live by what they teach us. We live by the joy, the worry, the anguish they give us and, sorry, we're in a bit of a trap there. And I think one can be honest about the trap, not pretend that human love, egalitarian justice, liberal dispensations, are very great creators of absolutely first-class work. They aren't.

This touches on one of the central concerns of your writing — the notion of answerability as an aesthetic openness to the text, to the otherness of the text, a certain mode of concentration, attention, vigilance. And there seems to be built into that word answerability, being responsible to the text, an element also of being responsible for the text, and by implication, for others. Now, this seems to me to be quite problematic — the claim that an aesthetic answerability to great works of art will lead, logically and emotionally, to a sense of moral responsibility. Yet the facts are otherwise. Very answerable people, in terms of artistic work, have been very morally suspect. How do you explain that contradiction?

Since we have so little time, let me try to answer you in two very simple ways. And the hardest thing in the world is to try to be simple on problems like this. Very roughly, Thomas Jefferson, Matthew Arnold, still a great teacher, F.R. Leavis, really believed that if you read better, you would vote better and treat other human beings better. I am simplifying, of course, but they made the link passionately, confidently — saying, you can't but be a finer human being, because your sensibility will be richer, more delicate, more apprehensive of the condition of others. In all my early work, when trying to show that people who could play Schubert like angels and read Goethe couldn't then torture other people in concentration camps, I came to the conviction that this was not demonstrable. On the contrary, as you've hinted before, sometimes, most awfully, the contrary prevails, and great readers are sadistic human beings or vote for fascism, and so on. Where is the bridge? In my more recent work, I've narrowed, I've tightened. That dubious figure and Titan among thinkers, Martin Heidegger who will, I think, dominate much of culture in the future, as did Hegel and Plato — not politically very reassuring either, by the way — Heidegger said, look, the great poet, the great artist, he isn't *speaking*, he is being *spoken*. Something we can express by a little English pun, he's being 'bespoken'. Something is passing through him. Something much greater than any individual. The language is greater than the individual, it chooses certain vessels to contain its glory and its radiant pressure. I'm now speaking in opposition to what is the prevailing fashion, the prevailing way of teaching, which says that anybody can rearrange what he reads. I'm protesting desperately against the posters on every single wall, where the conductors' names are much larger than those of the composers. I'm protesting against the producer thinking he's greater than Shakespeare, or Molière, or Aristophanes, when he has everybody naked, or in rubber masks, or on spaceships, doing classic plays. I'm pleading for a certain courtesy in the face of really great art. Put quite simply, the great poet doesn't need me. I need him. There is the picture of Pushkin in which he said, 'Look, I'm Pushkin. I'll give you the mail to carry. See that it gets to the right delivery box'. I love to do that. I'm not pushed when I can't do it, but I love to carry the letters, which is one way of teaching, one way of being, as you and I are, writers, critics, elucidators. It's a very modest function, but it has become certainly a dangerous and, I think, essentially a difficult one — to get people to *listen* at all, to *look* at all. But if you were to ask me does this carry the liberal, confident hope that you will then behave a little better in the street or in your home, I could not say I really have that hope.

If we could return to the notion of the European mind. You mentioned earlier that the Dark Ages of Europe was a misnomer, and you seemed to imply that pre-Enlightenment Europe was a time when people had a single culture, and that with the lingua franca *of Latin, they could move across borders and boundaries, and enter into some sort of social and political unity....*

You use the phrase '*lingua franca*'. There is no more deeper witticism or irony of history, and history is much wittier and more ironic than we are. *Lingua*, Latin. *Franca*, French. The two great moments when Europe thought it had a single language. And what is the *lingua franca* now? Anglo-American or American Creole or commercial American which organises the computers from Vladivostok to Madrid, the language every young scientist has to publish in, and has to know. I see a terrific contradiction, almost a trap. Can there be this new Europe when it speaks American? I don't know the answer, and I don't know anybody who has even begun to think this one through, because it's such a fierce challenge to all past history. What could be the basis for an answer? Could it be a revival of religion? Tricky one that. Fundamentalism is rampant again, not only in Islam, but also in Christianity. The Ukraine, which is one of the biggest nations on the globe, could again become a passionate Catholic wedge driven into the very heart of the Slavic world. Will we again have great religious wars? It's not excluded. One doesn't need to say this in Ireland where the sense of that is vibrant in the air. Is there another basis? I see only one. It is that of a shared body of active remembrance. When you visit Leningrad, whatever your feelings, you have twelve kilometres — it's scarcely imaginable — of cemeteries, of more than a million people who died of starvation and suffering in the siege. Right to the frontiers of Asia, which I tried to say are at Moscow, Europe shares a body of error, of remembered sorrow, of unspeakable self-destruction to the brink of suicide, in which there is perhaps also some hope. History might become the passport of shared identity, an actively lived and known history — and history is in many ways at the moment the dominant discipline of sensibility. We have lived through something so unspeakable. We were so close to the possibility of there being no Europe at all. And there's the re-entry of Spain — after forty years of Franco, we have one of the power-houses of liberal thought, art, philosophy and painting among us again, with its eagerness to join Europe, we're one of you: we too have lived that hideous history, of inquisition, and civil war, and Napoleon, and fascism. There are shared memories which an American does not share, which an Asiatic and an African does not share. They have their own immensely rich empires and evidences of the past tense. Ours is probably the most urgent, and there is at least a chance the young today are crossing borders as even you and I never were able to do, that there is somewhere a decision that that past *has to* have borne some very fragile fruit. Otherwise, the darkness at the back of us becomes even less endurable.

But the remembrance is one of our collective errors as much as one of our collective achievements.

There is a marvellous remark by the German poet, Rilke, that at the end of a good marriage one has to become the loving guardian of the other's solitude. I would say that at the end of an historic crisis one must become the loving guardian of one's own mistakes.

CHARLES TAYLOR is Professor of Philosophy at McGill University, Montreal. His books on the European history of ideas include *Sources of the Self; Hegel, the Pattern of Politics* and *Philosophical Papers*. Born of French and English parents, he lived and taught for several years in Paris and Oxford, where he was a founder of the *New Left Review*. He has been a key figure in recent debates on nationalism, federalism and bilingualism in Quebec, where he now lives.

CHARLES TAYLOR

Nations and Federations: Living amongst Others

Richard Kearney: *Do you think the transition to a new Europe involves a fundamental shift of identity?*

Charles Taylor: People don't have simple identities any more, they aren't just a member of their own nation. They have a complex identity where they relate to their *nation*, and their *region*, and they also have a sense of being *European*. They can exist on three levels. I think that is a fuller way of being, because it means more of your ties and connections are meaningful to you as against shutting some out in favour of simply one. And I don't think the old way of being, where everyone was locked into a Nation State with a sense of hostility to others is as good a way. Now, unfortunately, in Canada we may be going in the other direction.

You've had a federalist system in Canada.

We may be losing it now. Because some people can't somehow adjust to that and the strains may indeed pull us apart. But while this is a tragic development taking place at home, I'm really excited to see what's happening in Europe.

Could I tease out the parallels a bit? Some people in Europe at the moment looking to the history of Canada and America would say that the federal system in Canada simply didn't work, and that the United States of America, as a melting pot, is now in a situation where people feel they have no real identity, where there are high crime rates and drug problems, and indeed racial problems; and that if people don't have a sense of local attachment — or indeed national attachment to some sort of territory —

this leads to a lowest-common-denominator spiritless culture that ulti-mately issues in violence and war.

That's right. There are two kinds of federalism. We have to look at this. The United States is not the model for Europe, because the United States after the Civil War became what I want to call a homogenising federalist State. Culturally it's becoming more and more of a unitary State, even though it is constitutionally a federal State. The power is flowing more and more to the federal government. Canada, by contrast, had a real federal State, with real cultural homogeneity. Power wasn't flowing to the centre. The regional governments, the provinces, really had an import-ant role in people's lives. People identified with them. You can see this in the vote. The level of voting in democratic elections is high in Canadian provinces. It's very low in American States. It's even low in the American federal system. Now, Europe is plainly heading towards the Canadian kind of federalism. It's not going to try to homogenise cultures. It's going to bring together these different cultures, these different national identities. People are still going to be French, Irish, Italian and so on.

Well, you're optimistic about Europe, and I share your optimism, yet the evidence in your own country at the moment, particularly your own province, Quebec, would seem to suggest that that very federalism which you are invoking as a positive model for Europe is breaking apart at the seams, and that Quebec may well be, in the near rather than far future, a separate Nation State.

There are conditions for pulling this off, and we in Canada don't seem to have them, but you in Europe do. One condition is that people sense themselves happy with their identities, that they don't feel that their national identity is in some way put in the shade or looked down upon by others. You know, national identity is a very fascinating thing. In some ways, it's an inward-turning thing but in fact, deep down, it's an outward-turning thing. People want to be recognised by others. And when they feel not recognised, that creates the strains and tensions. We've never got over that, in French and English culture, in Canada.

You yourself are, as it were, a hybrid creature.

My mother was French, and my father was English, and I felt this all my life. Now, what's good about Europe is those strains existed within countries and not between them. Recently, one finds Corsican nationalism, or Breton nationalism, or Irish nationalism, a sense of pulling away within countries. The creation of Europe will allow those to find their own level without necessarily having to break up the units. Because as Europe is formed, paradoxically, the national State becomes less important and the region can become more important. And the national hatreds *between* European States, because of the bloodbath that ended in 1945, are so discredited that Europe can enter a phase where it's willing to put some of that behind it. So, because of this constellation of circumstances, you might say Hitler, on one hand, and more space for regional societies, on the other, I think Europe has a real chance of not breaking up the way Canada is. In Eastern Europe, you see something very different: and the old Soviet Union of course. They never experienced an aftermath of the Second World War in a free society where they could work out their reaction to it. The Communist governments were in a sense in a cultural deep freeze where nothing was worked out.

So the implication is that, if in the post-War era, the Eastern European and indeed Soviet Republics had been given the sort of autonomy and independence that the Nation States had in Western Europe, they too would be now ready to pool sovereignty and move towards a supranational federation?

Yes, we can hope so anyway. But we haven't had that. In some cases, there are very deep national hatreds, with recent massacres, you think of Yugoslavia — the Croats and Serbs; but in other cases, like Czechs and Slovaks, there's no reason why those two peoples can't fit together. They haven't massacred each other in recent history. And yet, it looks as though they too are under strain. And that simply is because they didn't have a chance, post-1948, to work this out in the way people in the West did in a free society.

It's been argued that a Europe of regions is all very well culturally or linguistically, where everybody can express themselves with their local colour, vernacular, rituals and festivals, but that when it comes to the hard crunch of economics, it is the centralised Nation State that still packs the punch. Of course, that is belied by the performance of Germany, Spain, Italy, France, and Denmark, who actually increased their GNP when they decentralised; whereas Britain, who under Thatcher, centralised power to an extreme degree, actually regressed in terms of economic performance.

The argument for central power is sometimes put in terms of controlling the economy, rather than just letting it go, and letting it prosper, having some input on it. But, you see, that tells also against the Nation State now, because the economic forces go way beyond the boundaries of the Nation State. That's why there's a case to be made for something at the level of Europe, and something at the level of the regions as well.

So economically speaking, there is not really any such thing as absolute national sovereignty any more.

No, no, it's less and less the case. And nations that try it on, like Albania, end very badly.

Well, if we could maybe pursue the British model a little. You lived there for several years, and taught in Oxford when Margaret Thatcher was the ruler of the land. As you well know, she issued, Cassandra-like, many warnings about the future developments of Europe. She dragged her heels and in the Bruges speech delivered a nightmare scenario about a Fortress Europe that would steam-roll national identities and subject us all to a mushrooming bureaucracy in Brussels. Do you think there is anything in that nightmare scenario?

Absolutely not. It's the reaction of a government that itself, paradoxically and strangely, wanted to control everything very firmly, and sensed that in a real federal system nobody controls anything very firmly, because control is split. I say 'paradoxically' because Margaret Thatcher, in some ways, passed for a political leader that wanted to get government out of society. And in one sense that was true — out of the economy. But the attempt to control things, the attempt, for instance, to take over local government, when it got in her way, to remake the whole local tax system from the centre in the Poll Tax, and so on, these were ways to get control over that society and remake it in the image of a certain ideology. People like that, ideologues like that, don't like federalism. It's the same thing with some of our separatists in Canada. They don't like federalism, because there isn't one place where there are all the levers that you can pull. I think that's really what it's about. So, it's quite the opposite of threatening a large bureaucracy in Brussels. It's the undermining of it.

Well, what would you say to those who suspect that the model of a federal Europe of regions is nothing but camouflage for a new Euro-empire to compete with, and ultimately win out over, the other great global economies and geo-political blocks — Japan on the one hand, America on the other?

Well, win over, I think that's not a danger. We're in a multi-centred world now where nobody is going to have the absolute advantage. However, I see one point in that criticism, Europe could become very inward-turned. And then we are in danger economically of trade blocs, like the North American trade bloc and the Japanese organising a rival trade bloc.

So there is the possibility of a certain European protectionism emerging.

There is a danger of that. But I don't think the lesson to be drawn from that is, let's not have Europe, because I don't think necess-arily that the Nation States of Europe have any better record of being outward-turned, if I can put it mildly, than Europe as a whole.

And maybe in any case we do need a certain amount of protectionism from Japanese cars and American pulp television.

Yes. And if there is going to be a war of the blocs, which I'd regret, Europe must be equipped to deal with it. But there is definitely a danger, the danger of a Europe that can't yet see itself as one great civilisation among others. The whole question of how to be one among others in the world today is a tremendous problem that nobody has solved, and everybody has to solve it in order to exist. It's the site of all sorts of neurotic hatreds and resentments. You look at it from the standpoint of Teheran, that is full of a sense of resentment at being put upon and despised by the West.

Europe too has its sins!

Oh, definitely. Europe has its complacency too, its sense of being still the definitive civilisation that everybody has to imitate, that doesn't need to learn about what's happening out there. That, of course, feeds into the attitude towards the large number of non-Europeans who are coming to live in Europe — the North

Africans, people from Turkey, South Asians, and so on. That is a very big problem. We have that in North America too. I'm not pointing the finger. All of us have to live in more and more multi-cultural societies, because the world is moving that way. And that raises the problem of being one among others, in an acute way, even in domestic politics, let alone in international politics.

There is an attendant fear that such a federal new Europe, based on a modern tradition of rights, going back to the French Revolution and the Enlightenment would in fact be a melting pot of atomized individuals, rather like America. This is another scenario often quoted, where the sense of social duties and commitments, fidelities to the common good of the community, of the nation, is actually traduced and travestied. Do you think it's a grounded fear?

It is. That's not because of Europe though. I think this is a grounded fear because the whole European tradition of rights is heading in the twentieth century in a certain direction which is potentially very dangerous. I mean, you're quite right there. On the one hand the European tradition of rights is one of the great realisations of European civilisation. I think the idea that a human being enjoys a certain indemnity where some things can't be touched and certain freedoms have to be accorded, is obviously a good thing...

So the danger is what?

The danger is that if that's the only way you conceive of political right it ends up drawing a fence around the individual and eroding the sense of individuals relating to larger groups, eroding, I would also say, the political process. What worries me about the American scene now is that the best and the brightest minds in America are concerned exclusively with fighting out the major battles in Supreme Court decisions. And the idea of fighting these battles by going out there and creating a majority and convincing fellow citizens to vote for Congress or the legislature, becomes less and less important, less and less vital. It gets to the point where a lot of people I know look at their Presidential candidate as a kind of three-quarters dead vehicle for the nomination of Supreme Court Justices when the next vacancy comes up. I mean, that's why a lot of conservatives rally behind Reagan or Bush. They don't admire these people — indeed, they think, in Reagan's case, he's almost brain dead — but they wanted him there because they trusted that when a Supreme Court Justice died off, he'd put one of their guys in and they'd turn around some of the decisions. Now, I think this is very unhealthy in a democracy, that the balance should go exclusively in that direction, and if I thought that the European Court would go in that direction too I'd be worried.

You are worried about too much power being given to a non-representative judiciary?
I'm worried about the political battles being fought out before the judiciary. That's not only bad because it disempowers the political process of majority voting, it's also bad because that way of putting these issues makes them into zero sum games. When you go before a judge, you are not asking for an intelligent accommodation, you're asking for what the law says. The law can say either A or B is right. It's really a zero sum game. And you get issues which could be intelligently accommodated if they were fought out between legislative majority and minority. When they are put before judges, it becomes all or nothing. Tremendous rigidities are introduced. People become shrill because they know they'll either get their whole point or they won't. The abortion debate is a good example of this. When people fight it out in terms either of the right of choice of the mother, which means no restrictions at all, or the right to life of the foetus, which means no abortion under any circumstances whatsoever, it's going to be *total* victory for one side or the other. Nobody can sit down and make an accommodation. On the other hand, if it's a legislative matter, then we're in the domain of a human political judgement which I think we ought to keep alive.

So that it is a question of balancing rights with duties.
Yes, a balancing of rights with duties with all sorts of other demands on us — not just duties, but the demands of decency, of harmony, of some kind of co-existence with our fellow-citizens. All these demands on us, as well as particular rights, can be put into an all-in judgement and worked out in real dialogue with real opponents, where you have to make a compromise, recognise

the other. That is the human process of politics, democratic politics.

But, grosso modo, you would say that the European legacy of human rights, which has given rise to the UN Charter of Human Rights, is a positive heritage.

Yes. It is, by itself, a wonderful heritage.

But it must be continually debated, interpreted, reinterpreted, to accommodate differing points of view?

Yes. It also has to be one element in a constellation. I would say the other part of the European constellation which is very great is democratic participatory politics. These two have to go together in a constellation. If ever one of them, like a cuckoo, takes over the whole nest and throws out all the other eggs, then you get a very unhealthy political culture, which I think the Americans are in danger of generating now.

Do you feel, at the moment, that there is an idea of Europe, a story of Europe, that is universal and that we can all tell ourselves, a guiding vision, a sense of direction enabling us to say we've come from there, we're here now and we're going there — or do you feel that such a Grand Narrative is no longer feasible and that we've got to treat Europe more as a patchwork quilt, as a medley of diverse voices and identities?

Well, in a way, neither of the above. The really healthy situation in Europe would be that everybody thinks there ought to be some kind of Grand Narrative, but there will be an intellectual contest over what it's going to be, and people are going to make *different* arguments for and against ...

So Europe should be cultivating a healthy conflict of interpretations which aim towards some kind of dialogue or accommodation?

Exactly. That's what you could hope for as the best realisable situation for Europe. If people came up with a grand narrative, and it fell apart into these unsuperimposable perspectives, without any relation with each other, then, you wouldn't have Europe any more.

You'd have a war between obscurantists.

You'd have a war between obscurantists, people falling into their own particularism — a little world where they don't care about the whole. Then you get into the kind of politics that emerges from an exclusive emphasis on rights where people say, 'I've got my demands and who cares how the whole picture ends up as long as I get my demands satisfied'. That's the mentality of people exclusively into rights, and organisations founded to get their rights. And that could be the outcome of the post-Modern Europe, where everybody wants their particular perspective re-alised and who cares about the whole. That's not a healthy political society.

It's a recipe for fragmentation and fracture without any sense of responsibility.

Yes. A deep sense of alienation from the whole. A sense of cynicism from the political process. In the end, if you like, an abandonment of solidarity. And I wouldn't wish that on Europe.

Is there a sense in which the genius, or positive heritage, of Europe has been a spiritual one which has been somewhat compromised by the contemporary movement towards secularisation?

I think that's true. I tried to discuss this in my book, *Sources of the Self*. I think a lot of even the most important streams of thinking of the European Enlightenment, or European secular humanism, have very deep roots in Christianity, Judaism, Islam, the things that are common to them. Very, very deep roots, which are not entirely overcome.

You argue that the sense of self is one of those, the sense of self-identity. Another is the sort of affirmation of everyday life.

Yes, the sense that everyday or, what I call, ordinary life, the life of work, of production, of marriage and the family, is something of ultimate significance. Here again, the ancients, Aristotle, for instance, had a view that what really matters in life was a range of higher activities, contemplation, or the citizen life, to which your life in the home and family or your economic life was simply an infrastructure which you had to have so that you'd carry on the really important things. And the revolution in thinking, sensibility and morality that's very much part of our modern age is an anti-hierarchical idea that a very meaningful part of human life consists of how you live your ordinary life, your life as a family person, your life as a worker in the economy. That's something which has very clear roots in Judaism on the one hand and Christianity on the other.

But you seem to suggest that in the modern invention of self-identity — of an inward, interior sense — there is also a continuity with a spiritual heritage.

Yes, because it's an origin point. I take St Augustine as my example. He's perhaps the best instance of a certain Christian line of thinking at the origin of much European thinking about the self. There interiority was not for its own sake, but in order to come to God. And something of that has remained in all the successor forms, even the secular, successor forms. It's something profoundly ambivalent — it can go in two directions. It can go in a direction which is totally focused on the subject, a kind of subjectivism — take its most important and obtrusive modern variant, the post-romantic idea that everybody has their own original way of being, their own thing to do, and that they have to find it themselves: they can't simply take it from someone else. Now, that's something which is a continuation of the idea of interiority. You find in yourself what your talents are, what you have a need to be. And that can take a very subjectivist form, totally focused on me, on self-expression. But it can also be the way that people discover their vocation to the universal, for instance, their sense that they ought to militate for ecological sanity, a sense of connection to the larger world, the larger nature that they have to fight for. It can take you in two directions, and instead of looking at it in a one-eyed way and seeing it simply as the added chamber to subjectivism, you can come to understand how it can be inflected in either way.

So it's not a fait accompli *either way. It's still a task.*

In modern culture, we can never get away from this modern insight that everybody has their own original way of being. That's very deep in our culture. But we can do two very different things with it. We aren't locked into one particular form, and that's important to see.

Finally, what would your hope be as an English-French-Canadian looking at Europe and concerned about Europe?

Well, in the immediate future, just that this movement towards a balanced federation would continue.

VLADIMIR VOINOVICH is a novelist. He
was exiled from his native Russia because
of his writing. Expelled from the Soviet
Union in 1980, he had his citizenship
restored by Gorbachev in 1990. Best
known in Europe for his biting satire, he
now divides his time between Munich and
Moscow. His books include *Moscow 2042,
Ivankiad* and *Pretender to the Throne.*

VLADIMIR VOINOVICH

Between East and West:
A View from Russia

Vladimir Voinovich: I am not a typical Russian. Maybe if you wanted some typical Russian, you'd have to invite Solzhenitsyn from Vermont. I would say that if Russians accept a new society with universal democratic rules they will also become a society of consumerism — because consumerism is, like it or hate it, natural for human beings. For instance, when I came first to Munich, the doorman of my hotel asked me, 'How do you find life here?' It was only my second day in Germany, my second day abroad at all. I said, 'I see very nice people.' 'Did you not see all those goods, luxury cars like Mercedes?' I said, 'All people like luxury goods. In Russia they cannot even dream about Mercedes, so they dream about Lada cars or Volga cars. But if they knew what a Mercedes was they would dream about a Mercedes or a Rolls Royce.'

Richard Kearney: So everything is relative. We're all materialistic, but some more than others: is that what you are saying?
Yes. The majority of people everywhere want to have a good life and to get these material things.

So you wouldn't share Solzhenitsyn's moral condemnation of the excessive consumerism of the West, where only that is good which is immediately consumable, immediately accessible?
Personally, I am also against consumerism, but I accept it because it's natural. It's inevitable. We just cannot avoid it. I also like to have many good things. I'm also a consumer. But I don't want to live in a society where consumerism replaces God, replaces religion. But I also guess that many people are against

it, people here are against it, but they cannot avoid this style of life. As in other parts of the world, this illness will defeat the Soviet Union too.

Laurens van der Post once made the remark that the USA and the USSR were the two lost twins of Europe; and he foresaw a day when Russia and America might once again return to Europe. Europe would be a place for the coming together of opposites. Do you think that reintegration of a split family is now about to take place, and if so, is it a spiritual process as well as a political one?

It's spiritual, it's political, it's natural. But I would say that between the USA and Europe, there is not as big a difference as between Europe and the Soviet Union. Not because of some sort of spirit of nations, but because of ideology. Soviet ideology was very hostile to other parts of the world. And many people are still keeping this hostility in their hearts. So we have to overcome this hostility. I believe that democracy, western democracy, is the natural state of life for any country. It is not ideal, but it's natural. In the Soviet Union, when they wanted to create an ideal society, they failed and they made a terrible society. But democracy corresponds to the people as they are, they can be good and bad but they have to live together. Bad people also have a right to live, no?

Would you agree then with those who argue that it is right to change the name Leningrad to St Petersburg, to try to reclaim even the spirit of Peter the Great who wanted to open Russia to the West, to Europe? Would you align yourself with that sort of openness to Europe?

Yes. I think it has to be, because without openness the world becomes more and more dangerous. And also I would say that all the countries have to use similar rules, similar laws for living together. Gorbachev would say, 'We will not be a western democracy.' But democracy is democracy. Western democracy doesn't exist. Democracy exists in the West, but it is not western, it is just democracy. And democracy is a natural genuine style of life. The Soviet Union has to accept this truth, and has to be, and all the countries have to be, like each other, to keep the same rules. Of course, all the nations are different but the main rules of democracy are necessary, like the rules of aerodynamics.

Basically you would say that it's not a question of Russia or the Soviet Union being westernised as such, but of them re-entering a world governed by universal rules. So it's not a capitulation of the East to the West. But could I bring you back to another warning note that was struck by one of your compatriots, Dostoevsky, when he argued that there was a great danger that the Slavonic spirit, which he identified with the Russian nation, was in danger of being compromised and contaminated by the introduction of Western European ideas. Would you have any sympathy with that particular nationalism?

No, no, no. I know this kind of thinking of Dostoevsky and of Solzhenitsyn also. But I absolutely disagree. This talk about a Slavonic soul, a Slavonic spirit, a special Slavonic nature, is just a legend.

Well, have they anything special to bring to a common European house?

Russia is now one of the very rare societies where people are still reading books. I don't know about Ireland, but in Germany, in the USA, in other countries, people are reading books much less now. In Russia people still read, and I think when they bring their traditions to Europe it will be a useful contribution.

That is a curious thing, because I think it's true in Ireland too that the poet, the writer, is often almost a national figure. I was very struck by the way, in the Soviet Union, that when a poet like Yevtushenko or Voznesensky gave a reading, or one of the exiled writers like yourself came home, the response was so amazing. People read your works. Practically three-quarters of a million copies of your last book were published there. And that culture of the book is, I think, something that our two cultures share. But if I could relate that to politics again — the key words of the Gorbachev regime which re-legitimised you, brought you back from exile and gave you back your citizenship, were Perestroika and Glasnost. Would you see those words, particularly Glasnost, as representing not just a political reality but also a spiritual, cultural movement?

Glasnost means freedom of speech at least. Glasnost brought freedom back to Russia, freedom to say or write anything. It abolished censorship.

And your own books are published again now.

Yes, my books are published. So I think it is very important. But in future this Glasnost, this freedom, may kill literature. Perhaps not totally, but ...

Are you saying that writers need a little prohibition or even persecution?
Not like it was before. But you know, literature played an
unusually big role before, because only writers were the people
who could say a little truth. And only they did it. And when it
will be a real freedom in the Soviet Union, a real democracy,
mainly priests and philosophers will take this place, replacing
many writers.

*In other words, the Russian writer was the conscience of the race or of the
culture, but because of the populism, and there is a huge popular following
for writers, you think that they may now be slightly compromised.*
The normal citizen in the Soviet Union could take his information about anything from fictional books, you know, sometimes
reading between the lines, sometimes directly, but only because
real journalism was forbidden, real philosophy, real religion was
always oppressed. So people had this cultural, spiritual, political
information only from books. Now books will not play such a
great role.

*Well, what about you? You've been accused of anti-Soviet activities, you
were expelled from the Soviet Writers Union in 1974, and eventually the
Soviet Union itself in 1980. You have been also accused of being a kicker
of sacred cows. When you returned to the Soviet Union and received your
citizenship back last year, did you fear that you might be domesticated,
that you might lose the satirical touch which has characterised all your
novels to date and become a mediocre writer?*
No. I didn't have this fear. When this process of Perestroika
started, many people said, 'Now, it will give no ground for satire.'
Yes, but now we have much more. Society becomes even more
funny than it was before. Before it was only the *caricature* that
was a target of satire. Now everybody is a target. Because people
try to adjust themselves to the new situation in funny ways, we
have even more subjects for satire than before. We still have
millions of readers and they will be devoted to literature for a few
more years. For me it will be enough, but in future the importance of literature will decrease.

*Your own favourite writers in the Russian tradition are Gogol and
Chekhov. Why those two? Is it the irony, the darkness, the melancholy?*

For me it's more the irony. When I was a young writer and wrote my first novel, I showed it to one old writer and asked him what he thought, if it would be possible to publish this novel. He read it and said, 'Yes, you will publish, but after that you will have a lot of trouble.' And I asked him why. 'Because what you are writing is so close to reality.' And so, I mean what I say. I did not want to satirise reality, I just wanted to depict it as it was.

And yet the orthodoxy of the Soviet Writers Union was socialist realism, that you simply hold up a mirror to the way things are. But they didn't like your particular image, did they?
No. They wanted to look at a mirror which depicted not reality but fantasy. The fantasy of Marx, of Lenin, and so on. And how reality has to be when this fantasy is put into reality.

But do you think there is a moral or religious role for literature? I'm thinking of the fact that the Kremlin was once the seat of the Russian Orthodox religion and of the Russian nation. And then it became the seat of a Russian empire. Is there not something in the spiritual legacy of Russian literature that can be developed and tapped at this point in time?
The Soviet and Russian leaders want it, of course. But they want to use this religion for their own purposes. Before they wanted to destroy it. But Russian literature wasn't always very religious. Dostoevsky, yes. Tolstoy, partly. He was also a heretic. He was expelled from the church. And Pushkin was not religious at all. Now many people in Russia say Pushkin was a very religious poet, but this is not so.

And what about Mandelstam and Mayakovsky?
Mayakovsky believed in secular religion.

But there was a zeal, a certain evangelical belief that the Russian soul could somehow save Europe and save the modern world.
Yes, many writers believed this. Dostoevsky and Gogol believed it.

Do you?
No. My attitude to this belief is ironical.

You're a sceptic.

Yes. I am a sceptic. When I see the people who now say, 'We are Russian, we will re-civilise the world', I take it in a very ironic way.

You sound a cautionary note.
Yes.

You're obviously quite suspicious of the possibility of a resurgence of Russian nationalism; and the way you talked earlier you would like to see Russia opening its doors to western democracy, or universal democracy for that matter. Have you got a certain ideal that you would like to see, not in the sense of blueprints that would be imposed from the top down, but as a writer and as a person? Have you got an ideal of a Russia that would have open boundaries, where people could migrate back and forth, as in a way you do between Germany and Russia at the moment, in a way that perhaps your own ancestors did when they left Serbia and first came to Russia?

Yes, you know, I believe the future of the world lies in all the boundaries being open; it will be like two oceans on different levels. And now the two oceans will want to be together. It's impossible just to dig a straight canal between them because that would be a flood. We have to build an irrigation system, where one level will be lower and the other higher, and finally these two oceans will be on the same level. It's very important for the future. The world will not survive without universal rules acceptable for *all* parts of the world. Because if we look now, we have many tensions between nations and countries, between societies and different social systems, many of them full of nuclear and chemical weapons. So there have to be similar rules. Hence my image of the two oceans.

It's almost like a canal system, as the levels are gradually brought together.
Yes, you know, when the ship goes from one sea to another on a different level, as in the Suez canal.

So the future of Europe will be governed by a sort of Boyle's Law of Culture.
The future of the world has to be. Now it is not so. If you opened the Russian border now, it would be like a flood. Life has to be everywhere almost on the same level. For instance, between here

and England you can go back and forth because the life is very similar: the quality of life. But some societies, like East and West Germany as it was before, had to build walls between them because it was impossible to live together.

What you're advocating then is a sort of homogenous European house where all the differences and diversities that make us interesting, culturally rich and non-conformist, may be lost?

Well, maybe one of the results may be losing some of these differences. But another result may be their preservation. For instance, in Germany, the Bavarians are still very much Bavarians and so on. In democratic countries people can save their national character much more than in totalitarian society. Hitler saw himself as a patriot trying to save the German character, but he destroyed it. Today people are learning to live together more democratically. Maybe it will lead to good. I hate all wars between nations, between different peoples. Our common goal is universality.

MIROSLAV HOLUB, from Czechoslovakia, is internationally known as a doctor and immunologist, as well as a poet and essayist. His recent publications in English include *The Fly, Poems Before and After, On the Contrary* and *Vanishing Lung Syndrome*. His bridge-building between the arts and sciences is virtually unique in European literature.

MIROSLAV HOLUB

Questioning Minds:
The Return of Middle Europe

Richard Kearney: *Has the role of the intellectual changed in Czechoslovakia since the 'Velvet Revolution' of '89?*

Miroslav Holub: Our activity may be different to the extent that we can now identify with the present establishment, which by definition is the intellectual establishment, it's a literary establishment. The President, and the most important personality of the country is a playwright, Václav Havel, and many writers and artists became very important personalities during the recent events in Prague.

And what does this do to you? Surely one of the roles of the poet in Czechoslovakia has been contestation, has been critique? What happens when that role of the poet as dissident, who says no — as indeed you do in the title of one of your poems, On the Contrary — *what happens when the naysayer becomes part of the establishment or leader of the country?*

Well, I don't know about the others, but for me the situation has shifted a little — there is no reason for me to say no to the present establishment, because I deeply believe this is a democratic establishment which has been elected, freely elected, and is continuing to develop democratically.

But isn't there some sense in which the imagination — the poetic or the scientific imagination — should always remain disestablished?

Oh yes, 'disestablished' is a beautiful word. Disestablished in relation to the old intellectual establishment and the reaction against the Marxist, Leninist, materialist 'science' of the Fifties, Sixties, Seventies and Eighties. There is a feeling now that we are switching or shifting a little too far onto the anti-scientific humanistic side of things. And science becomes almost a dirty word. Because I am not only a practising but also a believing scientist, I am in a position where I must disagree sometimes, or feel morally obliged to aim in a direction which is slightly different from the official direction in the literary world.

Given the fact that science was the official language and discourse of Marxist-Leninism and dialectical materialism in the Soviet Bloc, as in Czechoslovakia, what can someone in your position do to retrieve the name of science, and the positive role that science might play in the future?

Well, just to recall some very concrete facts. What was the real history? Of course the régime, the Communist régime, was using scientific or pseudo-scientific slogans at every possible step. Marxism was labelled the science of sciences until science was all over the place. And of course the organisation of science, the academy of science, was Party-dominated and Party-directed. The régime was the heaviest possible upperhand of the 'scientific' approach of things. Because it's amazing — this is not well known — but we had the bourgeois, western science, the 'wrong' science, and we had the *people's* science — the Russian, Czech, and Bulgarian sciences. This was the official attitude. In reality, the régime or the police disregarded the materialistic 'sciences of the people'. They always tried to steal some new technologies from the West. And what they also supported, under the surface, was all kinds of pseudo-science, occultism, alternative medicine, and so on. I know for sure because I was employed in a hospital, and some of the Party bosses always asked for healers, not for the official medical men, and they deeply believed in them. So, actually, the whole scientific approach of the régime was by this definition a counter-scientific movement.

In opposing those pseudo-sciences, those occult sciences, are you advocating a narrow description of science, mere analysis or mere description, or a broader approach?

By scientific approach I would define something that asks all the questions, not just some questions. You have to be, not cynical, but slightly sceptical about everything, including science itself. Actually, science is the only human achievement which is, by definition, by structure, *autocritical* — redefining, restructuring itself by its own free will.

*But isn't that the point where philosophy and science become reconciled
again? And that seems to be moving against the modern tendency to
separate them into two separate cultures — science on the one hand and
the humanities (philosophy, poetry and the arts) on the other. In your
attempt to bring together the scientific and the poetic imagination, do you
see yourself as retrieving a lost tradition, which in the Renaissance, the
Middle Ages, and going right back to the Greeks and the origin of Western
Europe, was a happy relationship between reason on the one hand and
imagination on the other?*

Well, in the Renaissance definitely, in the Aristotelian tradition,
or in the Greek-Roman tradition, to put it broadly, it was just
one thing — the fables of fables, science as well, and sometimes
including some types of rhetoric or literature.

*When exactly did that separation take place in the West, in your view?
And do you think there's any hope of undoing that gap or discrepancy?*

It may have happened during the first Industrial Revolution, in
the nineteenth century, it was shifting apart. But obviously it was
very much dependent on the structure of society, of the basic
economy of the society, where it was more outspoken or more
pronounced.

*So science became identified with the industrial devastation of nature. I'm
thinking of the criteria of industrial science by people like the romantic
poets, Blake and so on.*

Actually, I would say in a slightly cynical way that the split was
pronounced in societies which could *afford* it. With our Czech
enlightenment, with a national upsurgence, at the end of the
eighteenth and the beginning of the nineteenth century, there
was no such feeling because the nation was fighting for some type
of survival. I wouldn't say we were almost exterminated, but the
language was retreating into the villages, into the country, and
educated language almost didn't exist any more. It was lacking
in German, and so on. And under this condition, the redefinition
of the nation came in the same way in art, in poetry, and in
science. So that science was something which was deeply
identified with the national life. But the more we become a modern
society, the more we are setting these things apart, which is
obviously the 'two cultures' problem; it's a problem of affluent
societies, those that can afford it.

*It's interesting that some of the founding fathers of modern Czechoslova-
kia, I'm thinking of John Huys, the humanist theologian, and later again
Comenius, and later again Masaryk, the founding father of the present
Czechoslovak nation, were all to some extent questioning minds, they were
all scientists in whatever particular domain they worked — theology,
philosophy, education, art.*

This is a nice way to put it, the 'questioning mind'. I think that
the tradition of Czech Protestantism that developed with Huys
and Comenius, and continuing into the late nineteenth century,
was something which the Czech types of reasoning had in
common, and only in this century was it split into romantic
feelings on the one hand and scientific consciousness on the
other. I would think the peak of Czech thinking has been the
questioning mind.

*Up until this century then, science in your country was part and parcel
of the general culture?*

The man in the street would think of science in terms of the
Czech scientific tradition, the existence of the scientific establishment, like the National Museum, the Czech University. Even
in the late nineteenth century, the main struggle in science was
the struggle for Czech work in science, for a Czech science, in a
way. Now we are, of course, in the late twentieth century and
we are just going in the opposite direction. It's very hard to keep
your national or minority language in science, because there is
the one world language which is well adapted for scientific
purposes, even for the very essence of grammar and information
— the informational content of English is the biggest per unit
content. The rules of information are the simplest in English.
Therefore, it's the international scientific language. It's com-
puter-friendly.

*Czechoslovakia, at the moment, is witnessing a conflict of national
identities and cultures, the Czech on the one hand, the Slovak on the
other. What do you think should be the primary locus of identity? Nations,
regions, or the European federation that seems to be emerging now in the
extended European Community?*

This is a rather personal question. For me, it's not a geographical
position, it's not even the deep roots of Bohemia or Slovakia, or
the Czech kingdom, or whatever. For me it's the Czechoslovak

idea. Maybe it's not too rational, but I love Czechoslovakia without a hyphen. I just like all Czechoslovakia. Of course, I can't be against the federalisation of Europe, that would be very foolish and very conservative. Our aim and our hope is to be integrated, but to be integrated not as Czechs and Slovaks, I would prefer to be integrated as Czechoslovaks. We have Czech literature and Slovak literature. And in some instances we know the British or the Irish literature better than the Slovak literature, and vice versa. And we still translate from Czech. It's not necessary, it's like Scottish–English and English–English. It's not so different. But we still translate. We have all the news in both languages.

Are you Czech or Slovak?
I am a Czech. My second wife was a Slovak. But who knows what we are? I discovered one of my ancestors was a Mores. By definition a Mores was a Jewish name, so I don't know what I am. I don't care whether I am Czech or Slovak. For me, it's all the same. I regard being a Czechoslovak as my broader identity, but still a very definite identity, and, therefore, I would like to keep it as it is.

So, you're as mixed up as most Europeans today?
Yes, this is even a biological rule — the hybridisation, the change of the species is what counts. And, in this sense, even the diversification of the national identities in a unified Europe would be a positive biological trait.

You're suggesting that Czechoslovakia should be opened to this multiplicity of national and cultural identities. But would you go further than that and say that Europe itself, as an entity or an entirety, should be open to other cultures, to cultural differences that reside outside of its borders?
Europe is in a way all over the place. Europe is everywhere. Australia is not everywhere, Asia is not everywhere and China is not everywhere, but Europe is almost everywhere. And that's the trouble, how to define it. There are not clear European boundaries: this may be part of the legacy of Europe's colonial history. Europe is a very complex notion, and it is very hard to say how it will be influenced by other cultures. Europe has already influenced all the world, except for the most remote corners, very conservative, very isolated. I wouldn't say primitive. As America

has influenced the rest of the cultures of the world. Recently, I had the opportunity to see India, China, Turkey, and I was amazed that there are increasing numbers of American hotels, and of course, American tourists, and so some of the touristic pilgrimages are more or less American. In Istanbul, for instance, what is left of Turkey is the Blue Mosque, or the smaller mosques, and some of the poor of the street — the rest is Marlboro cigarettes, American tourists, American type hotels and so on.

How does one deal with this omnipresence of America in the world today?
There are two alternatives. We will maybe conserve our state, the face and the heart of the country, and we will stay poor, as in Asian countries. Or we will be Americanised, we will get all the dollars from the tourist traffic, but we will not look any more genuine. We will look like some kind of Disneyland.

But is there a sense in which Czechoslovakia can retrieve its traditional position as Mittel Europa, as the middle of Europe, both geographically and politically, and find a 'third way' beyond the polarities of East and West?
Years ago, even under the Russian boot, there was a Hungarian magazine which asked the question — is there a *Western* culture and is there an *Eastern* culture; is there an *American* type of superpower and a *Russian* type of superpower; and is there not something, a *third way*, a third type of culture, in a middle Europe? The result of the questioning was, yes, there is. Because everybody in Yugoslavia, in Poland, in Czechoslovakia would say, of course we feel we are different, we are different from both sides for good or for bad. For forty years, every man on the street has seen the wealthy German tourist in a Mercedes car become sort of a national dream. These people, plain people, would then go to Western Germany and buy fifteen-year-old Mercedes, which are hardly still going, and which will fall apart in the next year, but still they have a Mercedes. They look like a German, which is foolish, but with time they learn the other thing about the Mercedes — how hard you must work to earn one that actually works.

SEAMUS HEANEY

Between North and South: Poetic Detours

Seamus Heaney: If you grow up in Northern Ireland, you have the whole mind of Europe there around you. You have Iceland in the mission hall, the tin mission hall with the strains of Methodist song in the evening coming out over the fields.... When I went to Iceland I saw these little lonely tin huts in the middle of the tundra, and recognised Reformed Europe. So that Protestant dissenter's God is around you. The English God. A memory of the whitewashed chastity of Danish churches, all that. In Northern Ireland there is both this reformed Europe and then there is the pre-reformation culture of Catholic repositories, the Virgin and Child, the tawdry, 'dolled-up Virgin', as MacNeice called her. So, the Northern Irish mind is divided, or certainly embattled — if you're Protestant embattled by the Republic, if you're Catholic embattled by the Protestant thing — and that mind seeks ways in which to rephrase itself, make sense of itself, engender meaning out of confusion. And I suppose one of the meaning-seeking ploys that I used was to say that certain Eastern European writers — Poles and Romanians and Czechs — seem to understand these things better than English writers do. They take for granted disjunction, they take for granted that life will disappoint, that the roof is off the cottage of the universe. And I was being a bit unfair, of course. W.H. Auden recognised the roof was off, but he put it on again. But I would still say that people in Ireland have a greater sense of affinity than the English with that unsettled, uneasy, slightly distrusting attitude to reality.

Richard Kearney: *T.S. Eliot spoke about the concept of the whole mind of Europe. Do you think such a thing exists?*

SEAMUS HEANEY is an Irish poet. Born in County Derry in Northern Ireland, he has taught in Dublin and Harvard, where he holds the Boylston Chair of Rhetoric and Logic. He is also current holder of the Chair of Poetry at Oxford. His publications include several major collections of poetry as well as *New Selected Poems, Preoccupations* and *The Government of the Tongue.*

Well, I think it can be brought into existence, and it's thought to have been in existence. I suppose Eliot talked about it to some extent as an Anglican, a monarchist and a conservative. People in English culture like Matthew Arnold and T.S. Eliot promoted the idea of a 'mind of Europe' as an antidote to what they would have called provincialism, or Low Church life. I think that the tussle since Reformation times is to some extent a protest by the dissenter, the revolutionary, the protestant, against the totalising whole mind, the Latin mind, the imperial, big overall thing. It was a protest which said, let us have our own language rather than Latin, let's have the Bible in translation, let's have democracy rather than monarchy, and so on. So that the idea of a European tradition, the idea of European civilisation, these terms that were once hallowed are now suspect, because they seem to be imperial, totalising and Roman Catholic in a dangerous way. What the spirit of the age has in general promoted is a decolonising of the mind, taking out the big mind of Europe, putting in the mind of Ireland, the mind of Denmark, the mind of Spain, and so on. And of course it's correct politically to be on the side of decolonising your mind, and liberating yourself, realising that your consciousness has been to some extent created politically by big, totalising ideas. But, on the other hand, if you take out, almost in a military sense, the forms of the inheritance, if you take out Greek, Hellenic, Judaic culture — after all, the literary and artistic culture is almost coterminous with our discovery of moral culture, I mean, justice, freedom, beauty, love: they are in the drama of Greece, they are in the holy books of Judea — and if you take out those things, what do you put in their stead?

Well, you have local pieties, don't you? I mean, your own work started with a certain celebration of the country and countryside of Derry. Much of your early poetry was an exploration of the parish and all that it entails. Would you see a move in your recent work from this dissident, territorial, regional Heaney to a more universal, European, cosmopolitan Heaney?

Well, I wouldn't apply adjectives to myself like 'dissident' or 'European'. I'm just describing a movement of consciousness, a coming to awareness of what different myths entail. The Ireland and Irish literature that I grew up with and into were based upon pride in a kind of Gaelic Catholic difference, pure and simple-minded truths which are 'pieties' maybe: for example, Ireland was not invaded by the Romans, we had a Celtic background, we christianised Europe, we were not touched by the Renaissance, as Daniel Corkery proudly says. I did once regard all that as a sign of distinction in a good sense, but I'm not so sure any more.

What about your gravitation towards the Viking territory of imagination, particularly with the publication of North? *Wasn't there a sort of retrieval of another European geography there which might in some sense correspond to or complement the Northern Irish thing?*

Well, I think so, yes. The desire that one has is that what is possessed intimately should resonate more generally. You don't want to be promoting the local in its own right. I mean, the local has to be radiant with something you would call truth. And yet I'm not saying that when I began to use images of barbarous practices in Iron Age Europe, that I was self-consciously promoting the truth. I was just excited ...

You're talking now about the Bog People and the sacrificial rites of burial...

In the early 1970s, I made, as you say, this match, it's almost an intellectual rhyme between the sacrifice, violence and intimate killing in Iron Age Europe of a territorial, religious nature, and the territorial visions and religion implicit in Irish republicanism. So, yes, at that time I was, I suppose, in the grip of what is a romantic mythology — a sort of half-acknowledged presupposition that the nativist, the barbaric, is as authentic if not more authentic than the civilised; and then a moment came when I got a salutary reminder of what I was into. This was a moment in Macedonia. I went to a poetry conference, in Struga, and there was a Danish poet there. One afternoon, we went across the waters of a famous clearwater lake to an island which had the most entrancing Byzantine churches, monasteries with mosaics, those sages standing in God's holy fire, as Yeats said, images of the Madonna, of the Christ. And the Dane said to me, 'This is you, isn't it? You aren't really black bogs and sacrificial Iron Age creatures.' In a way he was right.

So your imagination started migrating from the North to the South of Europe.

Well, if you want to you can make a myth out of the authenticity, and the otherness, and the desirability of the Protestant North. And that is salubrious and salutary if it is to correct a rather too-smug idea of the absolute virtue of Graeco-Roman civilisation. But, on the other hand, I do think that you cut yourself off from enabling heritages and from visionary forms if you shut off what traditionally is European civilisation.

So, it's not an accident that your most recent book, Seeing Things, *marks a certain return to the vision and idioms of Homer and Virgil and Dante. What is it exactly in that Mediterranean, southern European thing that most fascinates you?*

I think it's a steadiness and a durability, a sense, for example, that in the word Orpheus, in the word muse, in the word drama, in the word mystery, or whatever, in the etymologies and associations, there is what Louis MacNeice calls a mystical sense of value. He said a writer didn't need to be a mystic, but it seemed to him that a writer needed to possess a mystical sense of value. And I do believe that in the English language, in the French language, in the Italian language, in the Greek language, and I'm sure in many other languages, these deposits do promote a quickening, a challenge. I'm not going to say a transcendent Europe of value, but the possibility of a hopeful, other, renewable, nonutilitarian, joyful spirit of being. Those promises, hopes and invitations reside in that Graeco-Roman-Judaic heritage, I think.

Well, to continue our magical mystery tour through the geography of Europe, having traversed the Northern, Protestant, Viking landscape, and said something about the Southern, Catholic, Graeco-Roman, perhaps you could now say something about Middle Europe. In The Government of the Tongue, *but also in other writings, you have shown a great interest in the work of poets like Mandelstam and Milosz, Holub, Herbert, Rósewicz, Sorescu. What is it about the East, and particularly Eastern Europe, that appeals to you?*

I think they speak the word, the original spiritual word, in a very laconic, down-beat, hard-bitten way. They combine, if you like, a Northern rhetoric which is saying no when it means yes, which is chaste, ironical and indirect, they combine that with quite a radiant desire for the big old values which were hidden erstwhile in big rhetoric. What you find in poets like Milosz, Sorescu or Holub is an invocation of classical mythology, not in a decorative, Miltonic way, but in a totally contemporary, angry way. I mean, Miroslav Holub has a poem called 'The Corporal Who Killed Archimedes'. Archimedes is working at the very edges, at advanced stages of mathematical and intellectual thought of his day, and the Corporal kills him, and then Holub says, 'And now he goes counting: one, two, one, two'. The Corporal has the power, but he doesn't have the creative capacities that Archimedes had. So for Holub, the classical past is a source of vivifying *exempla*. Again, Procrustes, the man who cut people to the same size to fit his bed, he's used by Zbigniev Herbert as an image of a totalitarian regime's ruthlessness in making everything uniform. Now, those are very snap examples. Much more important I think is the cherishing by those Easterners of what the West has taken for granted. We have become anxious in Western Europe about being Eurocentric, we have become anxious about the sins of colonialism. Even though in Ireland we think of ourselves as colonised, we too have after all connived in the imperial enterprise with our foreign missions, you know, to Africa. Of course it was a religious outing, but it was also an imperial outing, hand in hand even with the British Empire there. Nobody is free of self-blame when it comes to the abuse of European vision and fervour, but I think that that self-blame and that self-destruction of heritage has gone very far, and the East, among other things, reminds you that when the forms of value, when the value-engendering language is under fire, that heritage, the religious heritage, the cultural heritage, remains a possession. It's not just a stone-walling possession, it's something that is necessary to keep — humanist values engendering themselves.

This reminds me, Seamus, of one of the examples you touch on in The Government of the Tongue, *where you speak of a Russian poet, called Kutzenov, who buried his poems in a jam-jar at the bottom of his garden. This seems to be an analogy for the cultural memory that the dissident poets of the East have managed to preserve. Would you go so far as to say that they have preserved a more authentic and enabling notion of Europe than we in the West, with all our great rhetoric of European unity and community? Perhaps we need this reminder of cultural memory from Middle and Eastern Europe?*

There's no doubt that over the last thirty years, forty years, from Pasternak's *Dr Zhivago* and Mandelstam's poetry onwards, a certain voltage of joy about what is going on in the East came through. Now, it may be letting yourself off the hook to say, 'Oh God, aren't they marvellous? Look how they're resisting there.' So there has been a natural suspicion of this adoration of Eastern literature because it's a nostalgia almost. 'Isn't it great to have oppression. Look what a good literature it breeds.' Now, that is a kind of vulgarising of something that is genuine. I think that the Western intelligentsia is enlivened by the reality of spirit under pressure, by the spectacle of artistic and intellectual integrity. Words which the West had become shy of were still speakable in the East; and because they were speakable and manifest, it gave a certain excitement and joy to writers in the West. The problems of Westerners are, and were, different. It's a question of how to speak the utterly persuasive word in an atmosphere where no matter what you say it's not entirely persuasive. Our Europe stands between Eastern Europe and the United States of America, where the language has got a wide, wide weave, where the poetry, no matter how protesting — whether it's Ginsberg writing in the Fifties in San Francisco or John Ashbury writing in New York in the Seventies and Eighties — their protest is authentic, yet disappointed and hopeless; they would be shy of using a word like 'spirit', and if Socrates came into one of their poems, he would either be totally romanticised as a forerunner of William Blake or turned into a Donald Duck figure and ironised out of existence. That kind of ironical consciousness is what the West is used to, and so it got an injection of joy and a challenge to renewal from the East where poetry still had a close relationship to danger.

Several of these Eastern European poets have in recent history had quite an influential role to play in the reshaping of their own countries and nations. Havel is the obvious case in Czechoslovakia. But it's also significant that a poet like Dinescu was there in Bucharest when they took over the television station and proclaimed a free Romania to the world, or indeed that that particular rebellion was launched from Sorescu's own house, another poet. So, there seems to be a message coming through from

Eastern Europe that poets can play a reforming role in society. You have spoken about a tension between the command to engage actively in history and the need to contemplate the motionless point, to see poetry as its own reality. How do you respond to this message from Eastern Europe that the poet can have a public role?

There's no doubt that the poet can have a public role, but I think that the moment when the role becomes inevitable and compulsory is a special moment. In England in the seventeenth century, John Milton didn't bother his head with poetry for twenty years, it took second place to revolution, politics and religion. He wrote poetry as an exquisite attainment of a certain kind of civilisation up to his early manhood. Then, he put it away, and he was Cromwell's Latin secretary. Then, defeat, boom! — and he left. Milton is an example of the poet in public life yielding to an invitation to be a servant of something larger than art. In post-Romantic times, we have managed to unite the idea of poetic vision and national service. I mean, you had it in Ireland from 1890 until 1920. Poets made the 1916 Revolution. You had a sense of them being at the centre of power in a way that Havel and all these people are. But I think that when a society settles back (and, paradoxically, in spite of the Northern situation, you could say that there's an element of settlement about Irish society) then the role of the artist is oppositional. But it's oppositional in terms of modes of thinking, modes of apprehending. He or she can be the magical thinker, he or she can stand for values that aren't utilitarian. The artist can refuse history as a category, can say 'No. I prefer to dream possibilities'.

And is that a disruptive activity, to dream possibilities?

It is. It is a refusal of the terms. Take a poet in Ireland like Paul Durcan who seems to be connected up with the times: of course he is, but he's refusing the terms. In Durcan's case, what is dream-refusal can be taken for social comment. Of course it includes social comment, but its *modus agendi*, its way of going on, is to say 'I don't believe any of this'. If you take a completely different kind of voice like Paul Celan, you get a hermetic poetry, a secluded poetry, a poetry that huddles itself into the smallest space of language and says poetically within that language 'I refuse what's going on. I hate it.' So, artistic action is not necessarily dialogue, the much prized dialogue with other ideas.

It's a statement of 'Look. There is another way. We don't have to take this way of doing it.' Now, I'm not saying that all writing has to be like that, but I am saying that that's the nature of lyric for sure, it's the way a certain kind of abstract anger works in poetry, and it is sponsored by the dissident tradition in Europe also.

So you wc.ld be as suspicious of the poet king — the poet in power with maps and blueprints and dictats — as you would of the philosopher king.
I think so. There's been no example of a successful one. The poet Orpheus sings to the creatures and entrances them, and everybody goes 'ooooh', they just go into a trance. That's one kind of writing, the writer as entrancer. But that is not enough when it comes to the writer as an inhabitant of reality. And that's why Plato was against the poet, because of this entrancement factor, because the mind went to sleep and he went on automatic pilot as a human being. Now, the fully empowered artist, and the fully living response to art, goes beyond entrancement into what Yeats called the 'desolation of reality'. And there you have Orpheus, not as the puller of the harp string that puts everybody to sleep, but Orpheus confronting the fact of death and love, going to the underworld, always defiant but always failing to overcome death, always failing to absolutely make the perfection cohere. The possibilities within a culture, cultural inheritance if you like, are what mediate between the individual psyche and the uncontrollable size of the reality out there, the unknowable size of society. Cultural inheritance allows some form of negotiation to take place, to make sense of it all.

UMBERTO ECO is an Italian novelist and
theorist. He is Professor of Semiotics at
the University of Bologna and his books
include *The Name of the Rose, Foucault's
Pendulum, The Middle Ages of James Joyce,
The Aesthetics of Thomas Aquinas* and *Faith
in Fakes*.

U M B E R T O E C O

Chaosmos:
The Return of the Middle Ages

Richard Kearney: *You have argued that the 'Dark Ages' is a much maligned period of European history. Why?*

Umberto Eco: We can speak of the Dark Ages in the sense that the population of Europe lowered by twenty million. The situation was really horrible. The only flourishing civilisation was the Irish one, and that's not by chance. Those Irish monks went to civilise the Continent. But immediately after the Millennium, we cannot speak any longer of Dark Ages. You know that, about the tenth century, they discovered a new cultivation of beans, all those vegetable proteins. One historian called the tenth century, 'the century full of beans', it was an enormous revolution. Now, the whole of Europe started to be fed with vegetable proteins. A real, biological change. And the centuries immediately after the Millennium were called the First Industrial Revolution, because in those three centuries, more or less before the Renaissance, there was a larger scale application of the windmills, the invention of the new collar for horses and for cattle. With the old collar, they were practically strangled. With the new one, on the chest, the force of the animal was four, five or six times greater. Then there was the invention of the posterior rudder. Until that time, ships had a lateral rudder and it was very difficult to move against the wind. With a back-moving rudder, the possibility of a ship became enormous, the discovery of America by Columbus wouldn't have been possible without this technological innovation. And we can list tens of new miracles of discovery. So, it means that the European culture, the European society, grew with the new feudalism and the new bourgeoisie, the birth of

Italian and Flemish communes, the free cities, the invention of the bank, the invention of the cheque, of credit.

In one of your essays, you actually talk about the return of the Middle Ages. Do you believe that there is some sort of cycle to history, and that we are now reliving some of the traumas of the Middle Ages?

Well, in that essay I wanted to stress certain common elements in the sense in which our era is undoubtedly an era of transition, in a very accelerated way. It's enough to think of what happened in the last two years in Europe to understand the sense in which we are living in a new era of revolution. This is, as the Middle Ages was, an era of transition in which new forms, new social, technological, philosophical forms are invented. And at the time I wrote the essay I was also impressed by certain common patterns in the rise of terrorism: the Red Brigade and PLO etc. as a return of medieval millenarism, a sense of apocalypse and breakdown. The Atomic Age as a sort of reliving of the Middle Ages.

If I could take an example from literature now — Joyce, somebody you have written much about, including your book, Joyce and the Middle Ages. *You seem to argue that Joyce represents a balance between a fidelity to the cosmic order of the Middle Ages (represented in particular by his fascination for Thomist aesthetics), and an avant garde pioneering quality which you equate with the contingency and experimentation of modernity. Is there not a sense in which for you Joyce is an exemplar who combines a medieval aesthetic with a modern one?*

I think that Joyce is a paramount case of contrast and fusion, an incredible cocktail between those two aspects. They are present in his life in a Catholic milieu, the reading of St. Thomas Aquinas, a good understanding of it, and his interest in experimental literature, and this sort of destruction of language, that he called in *Finnegans Wake* the 'abnihilation of the ethym'. Joyce's work, as well as his life, was an oscillation, or dialectic between opposites. Take *Ulysses*. In *Ulysses*, he destroys all the existing forms of narrative, destroys all the existing forms of language. In doing that, he has built from the structure of the Odyssey, but it could have been something else, it was this medieval idea of the cathedral-like structure, and without this structure he would have been unable to undertake his work of disruption, destruction, decomposition. I think that this dialectic is present in every author, but in Joyce it was very evident and openly confessed by the author himself — the nostalgia for the order, the taste for the adventure, the necessity of using the order as a disruptive machine. That's absolutely new and Joycean.

So, you would argue that there is a dialectic between the nostalgia for a medieval order and a modern sense of chaos in Joyce?
Well, I chose as a subtitle of my book, *Chaosmos*, a word invented by Joyce in which you have this sandwich between *cosmos*, which means organised structure, and chaos. Obviously, an author who has invented the word *chaosmos* was a little obsessed by this possibility of creative opposition.

I'm reminded here of an example from your novel, The Name of the Rose, *where the hero, the monk, is wandering through the labyrinth of the library, and he comes across a forbidden section where books on comedy have been hidden away. The point seems to be that while the western tradition, and the western church in particular, allowed Aristotle's teachings on tragedy, it censored Aristotle's writings on comedy; and in this secret section of the library, you also have a series of commentaries by Celtic, Gaelic monks full of the paraphernalia of the Book of Kells — humour and mischief, contradiction and conflict. Are you making a point here about a certain Irish openness to contradiction and humour?*
You know, the Middle Ages was a serious Age, because it was an age of faith and such things, so that the subject-matter of every discourse was God. It had to be serious. But since it had also a great sense of humour, it was also an age of carnival and of popular licence. It is enough to read Chaucer or Boccaccio to understand that they were not as virtuous as it seems. They tried to exploit this. The Margins. There is a form of decorative art called Marginalia. The texts were dealing with divine martyrs, and the Margins were a sort of amusement, inventing, quoting from fairytales, from popular legends. What happened with the Irish medieval culture was that *Marginalia* became *Centralia*. The Book of Kells is made only of Marginalia, and that is the way in which Irish culture was already Joycean at that medieval moment, trying to introduce extraneous elements, to disturb the order of things, to find a different order.

You've argued that Finnegans Wake *tells of the quest for a universal language — or to be more accurate, a parody of the old traditional quest for an original tongue, some kind of alphabet that would pre-exist Babel and the division into multiple tongues that today make up our polyglot civilisation. Now, your point seems to be that there is no such thing as a return to a time before Babel, that we live in a post-Babellic age, to use your phrase, where it's the very multiplicity, plurality, confusedness, and complexity of languages, that makes us what we are and is perhaps our greatest virtue.*

Well, the story is the following. For two years I've been working on this extraordinary episode in the history of European civilisation — the quest for a perfect language. Before the birth of Europe, there was not such a preoccupation, because the Greek civilisation, or the Latin civilisation, had their own language, which was considered the right one, and all the rest was considered barbarian. (The term 'barbarian' originally meant stutterer, people unable to speak, without a language.) As soon as Europe discovered the plurality of new languages, they started dreaming of some kind of universal language. There were two options. One, to go back before the confusion of the Tower of Babel where, according to Genesis XI, God confused language. Before, there was a single perfect language. And so there is in European history this effort to return to the purity of the original Hebrew, or another pre-Hebrew language, the one used by God to speak to Adam. And the other attempt was, on the contrary, to build up a new language that would allegedly follow the rules of universal reason — a language that could be spoken by everybody. Both were attempts to heal the wound of Babel. But there are, in this history, other such efforts. I discovered recently, probably one of the first texts about the story of Babel is an Irish drama of the seventh century in which it is told that the Gaelic language, invented by seventy-two wise men, instead of trying to go back before Babel or to eliminate the plurality of the other languages, tried to pick up the best from every language to create a perfect Irish language. This mythical idea seems to me very similar to the idea of Joyce, who dreamed all his life of an alternative poetical language — *Finnegans Wake* is a proof of it. He did not try to invent a new one, or to rediscover an old one. *Finnegans Wake* is not written in English, it is a sort of polyglot construction in which every possible type of language is contributing to a new kind of discourse. What is the meaning of this metaphor — which is a metaphor, obviously, because it's impossible to think of a future Europe speaking in Finneganese? It is probably that the future of Europe is not to be seen as a development under the standard of a unique language, such as Esperanto, but as a sort of acceptance of a civilisation made of various languages. In Europe something different can happen, unlike what happened in the United States where the unification was made under the heading of a unique language.

English?

Yes. There were French-speaking people, German-speaking people, Dutch-speaking people, and all of that, but English became the unifying language in America. In Europe, we are facing more and more a fragmentation of languages. Look at what is happening in Yugoslavia. Or in the former Soviet empire. Lithuania, Estonia and Croatia are becoming again official entities. If today we could think of a Europe with three, four, five languages, the Europe of tomorrow would have tens of different languages, each of them recognised in their own autonomy and dignity. And, so, the future of Europe is probably to acquire a sort of polylingual attitude. And there is in the universities at present an interesting sign of this. It is the Erasmus project. I have always said that the most important feature of the Erasmus project is the sexual one. Because, what does it mean if every student is supposed in the future to spend one year at least in another country? It means a lot of mixed marriages. It means that the next generation will be largely bilingual, with a father and mother from different countries. That's the best chance for Europe.

So, you're really talking about exchange, inter-change, confusion in the best sense of the word. It reminds me indeed of something that Brian Friel, one of our Irish playwrights, once said in his play Translations, *that confusion is not an ignoble condition.*

No. It's the original condition of the Cosmos. Before the Big Bang there was a great order, and a great peace. The Big Bang was the beginning of the confusion in which we live.

But isn't there actually a stronger claim in what you're saying. I'm reminded of your argument that if God spoke to Adam he spoke in Finneganese.

It was again a metaphor. But yes, the idea of a perfect language is a Utopia. If it is possible, I don't say if it's true, to think that evolution took place several times in the world in different places, it is also possible to think that language was born several times in several places. The idea of an ideal language is that there was first a speaking animal, then all the other languages derived from it. And so it was for centuries, they dreamt of Hebrew as the original one, and then of Indo-European, and so on. Mankind being a speaking species, it is probable that languages were plural from the beginning. And seeing that plurality is a natural condition, it would be artificial and inhuman to reduce this plurality to an impossible unity.

To take this back again into the realm of Europe, aren't you really claiming that cultural contamination is a good thing, that we should be muddying the waters, mixing together different languages, different races, different nationalities, and that one of the great errors of Europe has been the attempt to fashion some kind of purity of culture or politics? Two indications of this might be, on the one hand, the tradition of the centralised nation state which suppresses its regional minorities and languages — in other words, refuses in its rage for uniformity to acknowledge the existence of a plurality of cultures within; and on the other hand, the attempt to close the frontiers of Europe and see it as some kind of ethnocentric, privileged continent which can deny all those influences from Asia, North Africa or the Americas, which have made us what we are. So could it be said that your basic argument is for a Europe of open frontiers which would see the confusion of different identities and languages as something positive?

I dislike the use of terms like 'should' or 'would' that imply a certain will and intention. It is irrelevant what Europe wants or doesn't want. We are facing a migration comparable to the early Indo-European migrations, East to West, or the invasion of the Roman Empire by the Barbarians and the birth of the Roman-German kingdoms. We are not just facing a small problem of immigration from the Third World; if that were so, it would be a problem for the police, for the customs, to control. The new migration will radically change the face of Europe. In one hundred years Europe could be a coloured continent. That's another reason to be culturally, mentally ready to accept a multiplicity, to accept inter-breeding, to accept this confusion. Otherwise, it will be a complete failure.

One thing that comes through in nearly all of your work — your fiction and your critical writing — is a wonderful sense of humour.

I think that a sense of humour is a healing quality in every culture. When there is a total absence of humour, we have Nazism. Hitler was unable to laugh. It's not only a European problem. I think that there is in humour, in a serious practice of humour, a religious effect. We are small creatures, we need not take ourselves too seriously.

JULIA KRISTEVA is Professor of Linguistics at the University of Paris VII. Born in Bulgaria, she came to study in France where she quickly became a celebrity of the avant-garde 'Tel Quel' group. Her publications include *Revolution in Poetic Language; Desire in Language: A Semiotic Approach to Literature and Art; Powers of Horror; In the Beginning was Love: Psychoanalysis and Faith; The Black Sun; Strangers to Ourselves* and a novel, *The Samurai.*

JULIA KRISTEVA

Strangers to Ourselves: The Hope of the Singular

Julia Kristeva: I consider myself a cosmopolitan. I was lucky in my childhood to learn French at an early stage. My parents sent me to a French pre-school in Sofia run by Dominican nuns: it was an offshoot of the Jesuit college in Constantinople. So I started French before my Bulgarian studies. Then those ladies were accused of spying and expelled from Bulgaria. Their work was taken over by the French Alliance. So I learnt French at the same time as Bulgarian and my entry into French culture was somehow a natural one. When I arrived in France to pursue my third level education, I felt that I somehow belonged to the French culture — which is not the case seen from the French side for they still perceive me as a foreigner although I was very warmly welcomed.

It is easier to consider oneself cosmopolitan — as I do — if one comes from a small country like Bulgaria, just as it is probably easier to be European when one is born, say, Dutch, than it would be if one is English. I insist on this point for I believe that the future of Europe lies in this idea of respect between nations, but also of conciliation between nations. I care very much for this cosmopolitan idea which is a heritage of the European culture of the ancient Stoics, later developed by French thinkers of the eighteenth century. I take this cosmopolitan idea of the enlightenment very much to heart, and if there is hope for Europe, beyond the ethnic conflicts that are breaking out today in Yugoslavia, Czechoslovakia, Romania, Bulgaria, the Soviet Union etc... it is in this spirit of universalism. We must move beyond nations, or archaisms, while also recognising genuine particularities.

Richard Kearney: *Another word on Bulgaria, your own native land, and so-called 'Eastern Europe'. How can we relate to this lost or amputated part of Europe?*

I don't experience this dichotomy of the two Europes in such a pained manner, for two reasons. First, for biographical reasons which I already mentioned, that is my early entry into French culture; but also because I have made an intellectual choice which consists in thinking that the origin is not essential, that the origin is a reaction to pain and can become a condensed brew of hate. People who turn back to origins are people who don't know how to metabolise or sublimate their hate, they are wounded people, depressed people; and because they no longer have ideals — religion does not satisfy them, nor does Marxism, and no other providential ideology can come to their rescue — they turn towards the archaism of the origin. My entire intellectual education goes against this idea of origin.

Is it feasible, or even fair, to dismiss the complex reality of nationalism in this way?

I do recognise that we are going to live for a very long time in the frame of nations and nationalities. I am against that tendency of the Left to dismiss the idea of nation. I believe the idea of nation is going to have a long life. But it should be a *choice*, and not a reflex or return to the origin. When one lives it as a choice — that is to say with clarity of vision, knowing the political, ideological, cultural reasons that make us adhere to France, Ireland, Great Britain etc, and not because we are genetically linked to it — it can be a good choice.

So to come to the other aspect of your question: what can my experience of the East give me today? I believe two things: firstly, an ability to winter out, to acknowledge the importance of effort. We were children who suffered quite a lot of economic deprivations (although they weren't disastrous, especially at the age I was). So we have been pushed into giving the maximum of ourselves; and those who weren't able to step over this threshold of discipline and endurance were swept away. This gave us a hard-learnt power to concentrate and be disciplined. Secondly, I learned from Bulgaria the importance of *culture*. Bulgaria is the country in which the Slavonic alphabet was created. It was two

Bulgarian brothers, Cyril and Methodius, who gave the Slavonic alphabet to the world — it is now the alphabet that the Russians use. There is in Bulgaria a Feast of the Alphabet, probably the only one in the world. Every year on May 24th, children parade in the streets of Sofia each displaying a letter on their fronts, so we are identified with the alphabet.

So the famous Cyrillic script was originally Bulgarian.
Yes, Saint Cyril gave his name to the alphabet. There are discussions still going on about whether he was Greek or Bulgarian; his mother was of Slavonic origin, he knew the Slavonic languages, and when the Pope asked for the Gospels to be translated into Slavonic to evangelise the Eastern nations it was the two brothers, Cyril and Methodius, who were sent on the mission.

So in Bulgaria there is this pull to identify oneself with culture which I experienced very vividly in my childhood as a positive element, and I believe that many people in the East, especially students, have a cultural avidity and curiosity that western youth has lost because it has a surfeit of culture (you can buy anything anywhere for your bookshelf), and because the mass media have destroyed the taste for classical culture and great modern culture. Europe is going to suffer the dissolution of culture for a long time to come.

I have just finished writing a novel called *The Old Man and the Wolves*, in which I tell the story of the brutality of the modern world which one can find as much in Ireland and Great Britain and France as in Eastern Europe. There is a crazed fashion: violence against people, lack of culture, lack of respect, and it is getting worse today with the collapse of the pseudo-classical culture, nothing is left. It is something we will find very hard to get through. There will be two big problems — the market economy, and the need to climb up the slope of fifty years of cultural and moral emptiness. We also have a lot of work to do as intellectuals, for example, in helping with cultural exchanges at the level of the humanities.

I would like to ask how you combine your cosmopolitanism as a French citizen with the fidelity to your place of origin; and by extension, whether some recognition of national or regional origins isn't necessary. You suggest that nationalism is a pathological symbol, but does it not only become that if we ignore the basic human need for a certain national identity?

Baltic, Serbian, Slovak, Croatian nationalism is, in my eyes, a regressive and a depressive attitude. If you'll allow me this little psychoanalytic excursion, these separatist nationalists are people who have long been humiliated in their identity. Soviet Marxism did not recognise this identity, so they have now an anti-depressive reaction which takes manic forms, if I may put it like that. The exaltation of origins and of archaic folk values can take violent forms because one wants an enemy; and as the enemy is not communism any more — because it doesn't exist — the enemy will be the other: the other ethnic group, the other nation, the scapegoat and so on. This pathology can last for a long time and such archaic settling of accounts can prevent, or certainly handicap, the economic and cultural development which those countries need. One can try to accelerate the process, one can try to avoid sinking into stillness, to help it go a bit faster; and at that level, there is a huge amount of work that can be done on one side by the Churches and on the other by the intellectuals. It seems to me that in Eastern Europe, the Catholic Church played a major role in the rebellion against communism. It has a great role to play today in helping to transcend nationalism and to give to those people ideals which would not be strictly ethnic or archaically national. Recently the Church wrote an encyclical which shows it to be extremely interested in the moral struggle against totalitarianism but also against a certain 'Americanism'. I am quite struck by this cosmopolitan and Universalist idea of the Christian Church as a remedy for those nationalisms that one shouldn't dispose of too promptly, but should try to transcend.

If the crisis is not only political, but moral and spiritual as you suggest, doesn't that mean that the solution must also be of a moral and spiritual order?

Even economic problems cannot be solved without this moral renewal. Imagine people who must face a market economy based on the idea of individual competition while their sense of individuality is still extremely weak, wounded, frail. In order to consolidate this sense of one's individuality, of one's autonomy, of one's freedom, one needs a great moral support. That is why I think that those two aspects, the economic and the moral, are linked together. I would give priority to the moral revolution.

Are you advocating therefore a return to nineteenth-century liberal humanism and individualism — I am thinking of the legacy of Locke, Hume and Mill in particular who advanced the idea of individual rights outside of a communal or social context? Or is what you're talking about something that goes beyond traditional individualism towards some new right to singularity compatible with social solidarity?

In my view, it is a right to singularity. But it is not obvious that they will be able to achieve this singularity, coming from an ideology of collectivism, unless they go through some form of individualism.

Is it the old liberalism of Locke and Hume, that you are advocating?

It is not rampant or uncritical liberalism. This why I insist on those better forms of individual identity that one can find in religion and in the Enlightenment. Here I quote a phrase that appears to me to express the aim of Christianity even if it goes far beyond it. It is from Montesquieu's *Pensées*, and goes something like this: 'If I knew something that would be useful to myself, but detrimental to my family, I would cast it from my mind. If I knew something that was useful to my family but detrimental to my country I would consider it criminal. If I knew something useful to Europe, but detrimental to humankind, I would also consider it a crime.' It is a very interesting idea because it recognises the individual, the person, the family, the nation — but it also considers that the individual person can only find its development in a wider frame.

Is this what you would call the cosmopolitan model?

Yes, because the nation, the individual, the family are recognised as transitional objects, to speak like Winnicott, as moments of consolidation which are necessary but not sufficient. It is this transitional logic that Montesquieu develops in this saying. And I consider that it should be studied in all French schools because it is not clear that all French people apply this logic, far from it. There is difficulty in living as a foreigner in France. Above all it is something we should try to share with our friends from the

East, so that both their ethnic belonging and their nation are recognised, while encouraging them to avoid fixations and limitations at that level, to move forward towards wider horizons.

Are you suggesting that religion could play a positive role by going beyond particular denominations or sects and projecting some common universal content? Do you see that positive role as operative today?

There is a homogeneity in particular religions which makes you into a stranger if you don't share their presuppositions. That said, our monotheistic religions have tried to develop a notion of the Other, and it is that point which seems to me a totally exquisite point of western thinking that we should enrich and cultivate, that the Enlightenment tried to extrapolate, and that it is part of our inheritance to develop. What does that mean? When a stranger knocks at my door, for instance, I should, as the Bible says, consider that it might be God — a sign of the sacredness and singularity of others. It also means that, as the pilgrimages from the first centuries of Christianity until Saint Augustine taught us, the journey, the idea of carrying the message of Christ towards others and of receiving strangers coming as pilgrims, leads to a kind of osmosis between ethnic groups. The idea of *caritas*, Christian love, of which we know the degenerative form in the horrible history of western colonialism, gives a strength today to the Christian churches. We can see it being developed, for instance, in 'le secour catholique', or other forms of action which Christians in France organise for foreigners: teaching migrant workers and their families how to read, material aid, etc. I believe it is important to focus on this aspect of religious movement in so far as they have a popular audience and can respond to the dangers of narrow nationalism.

Once religions have done that work is there not another kind of work that remains to be done?

Alongside this work, there is much to be done at the level of the individual, developing the dimension of singularity. Our ideas don't fall from heaven, we have a heritage, and we must bank on it; otherwise we become abstract. There is a radical change which occurred in the eighteenth century in our understanding of human singularity; and there is also much to be done through psychoanalysis — something I am committed to in my daily work.

Are you suggesting that this work on the private realm of the psyche cannot be properly exercised by politics or religion but only by psychoanalysis, a work of the soul?

I am not going to preach psychoanalysis. For the analyst, the person who comes to analysis is a person who must express his or her own desire for it. So I am not going to suggest to your viewers to start analysis. But I believe that psychoanalysis is a modern form which takes into account the Jewish and Christian monotheist heritage and the Enlightenment knowledge of the self and of our singularities. But it is possible to find other forms of learning more about this singularity which range from personal meditation to art, reading, music, painting.

Is it possible to achieve this through the relationship with another person?

For me the relationship with another person is essential. As forms of sublimation, the arts are often extremely important, but also sometimes very dangerous because they are insufficient. They can lead someone to become complacent with singularity, they can lead to closure rather than to an overcoming of malaise. So, yes, relating to others is indispensable to the development of singularity.

Finally I would like to ask you what you feel is the role today of the great European project of the Enlightenment? I am thinking of Voltaire's and Montesquieu's dream of a great European cosmopolitan republic. Since they first expressed their vision, we have witnessed not only the breakup of Europe into rival nationalisms and Nation States, but also two world wars in our century which were a direct result of such antagonisms. After those two world wars, and after Auschwitz in particular, what can we advocate today as a viable and legitimate project for a united Europe?

We have to take seriously the violence of identity desires. For instance, when somebody recognises him or herself in an X or Y origin, it can appear very laudable, a very appealing need for identity. But one mustn't forget the violence behind this desire. This violence can be turned against oneself, and give rise to fratricidal wars. So what we learn is the relativeness of human fraternity and the interest, not only pedagogical but therapeutic, one should take in the death wish, in the violence within us.

How fraternity can become fratricide?

Exactly. Therefore, along with the care that one should give to the death wish, there is a need for a lot of finesse in the way one deals with individuals, but also with their relationship to nations. After the Enlightenment, the idea of the nation was for long considered a backward and archaic idea that one could brush away, do without. I believe that, at least on an economic level, the nation is here to stay; we will have it with us for at least another century. But it is not enough to realise its economic dimension; we have to measure the psychic violence of the adherence to this idea. This is a violence that can also be carried by religions, for religions can be another form of originary adhesion. The shapes of fundamentalism that spring up nowadays on all sides cannot be dissipated simply by fraternal good will. One is going to encounter a lot of difficulties. We are faced with a death wish. I believe the closest we've got to it was after the fall of the Berlin Wall. When that happened, whatever screen hid us from this death wish fell. The screens of new Promethean ideologies, like Marxism, don't exist any more. The old religions, even if they are still solid and will endure for a long while, are being put in question. Nothing can wipe out or hide this death wish. We are left face to face with it and the most adequate response to be found is, in my view, the sublimatory and clairvoyant forms that art and psychoanalysis represent.

The media propagate this vision. Look at the films people like to watch after a long tiring day: a thriller or a horror film, anything less is considered boring. We are attracted to this violence. So the great moral work which grapples with the problem of identity also grapples with this contemporary experience of death, violence and hate. Nationalisms, like fundamentalisms, are screens in front of this violence, fragile screens, see-through screens, because they only displace that hatred, sending it to the other, to the neighbour, to the rival ethnic group. The big work of our civilisation is to try to fight this hatred — without God.

EDWARD W. SAID

Europe and its Others: An Arab Perspective

Richard Kearney: *As an outsider looking in, do you think there is such a thing as a distinctively European tradition?*

Edward Said: I think there is no question but one can talk about a European tradition in the sense of an identifiable set of experiences, of states, of nations, of legacies, which have the stamp of Europe upon them. But, at the same time, this must not be divorced from the world beyond Europe. In the Algerian context there is a good phrase for this — 'complementary enemies'. There is also a complementarity between Europe and its others. And that's the interesting challenge for Europe, not to purge it of all its outer affiliations and connections in order to try to turn it into some pure new thing.

What is becoming of the 'European intellectual' today?

The idea that the intellectual is a professional who is rewarded for his or her services has meant in the United States and in Europe that you have this extraordinary gravitation towards centres of power, that the intellectual thinks that the reward or the goal for what he or she does is a policy playing, a policy forming role, to be an opinion maker, a policy maker. Whereas my view is that the intellectual role is essentially that of, let's say, heightening consciousness, becoming aware of tensions, complexities, and taking on oneself responsibility for one's community. This is a non-specialist role, it has to do with issues that cut way across professional disciplines. Because we know about professional discourse. I mean, it becomes a jargon, speaking only to the informed, keeping them essentially in a state of acquiescence, and promoting one's own position in the end. That's something I find deeply

EDWARD SAID is a Palestinian critic and author who has lived and taught most of his life in Europe and America. He is currently Professor of Literature at Columbia University, New York, and his books include *Orientalism, Covering Islam, Question of Palestine* and *The World, the Text and the Critic.*

abhorrent, because it seems to me that society is made up of two kinds of people. There are the maintainers, the ones who keep things going as they are, and there are the ones who are the intellectuals, who provoke difference and change.

And you would introduce here an ethical scruple of responsibility for one's fellow-citizens.
Yes, I think that's the essential thing.

And if that means a contamination or confusion of realms, then so be it?
So be it, exactly. For me, what has been terribly important is that I have a sense, maybe it's an accident of birth, that I'm affiliated with a national community — Palestine. Partly because of the universality of the cause, Palestine is not just a simple nationalist struggle, it involves the cultural problem of anti-semitism. We have become the inheritors of European anti-semitism: we are the victims of the victims, if you like. It's a complicated role. Nevertheless, having some connection with a national community — or community, never mind national — keeps one honest.

But is this where you would see a social and moral role for the intellectual, where in inventing or reinventing our traditions, we can actually take apart and analyse the myths and the symbols? There's a lot of talk at the moment about the creation of a new Europe. Do you think there might be a danger that we could witness the emergence of a new form of cultural imperialism?
I think the likelihood of a kind of imperialism that one associates with nineteenth-century European imperialism is not very great. And I think the overshadowing power and influence of the United States is also a kind of impediment to it. One would like to think that Europe — at least that's the way I think from the point of view of the Arab world — is a kind of counter to the United States; that it provides, partly because of the Mediterranean links between some of the southern European countries and North Africa, a kind of exchange of cultures that is not imperial, and that there is more give and take than before.

But has Europe succeeded in acknowledging the other in its midst: the traditional other, in this instance, being the Arab or Islamic world?

No, I don't think so. I think there's a problem. Take Italy. Italy now sees itself as saddled with about a million Moslems, all of them from North Africa, largely from Libya and Tunis, some from Egypt. This is unacknowledged, as opposed to France, which has also two or three million Moslems, which is a political issue. But I think discussion and debate, even the kind of rancorous debate that you get between Le Pen and some of his more liberal opponents, is better than the silence you find in Italy. Nevertheless, there is a presence there which is going to provoke more discussion and more awareness. And, interestingly enough, there is now in the Arab world a set of writers, thinkers and intellectuals who are very serious about a Euro-Arab dialogue, exchange between the two that will break down some of the hostility, the kind of blanket, 'Arabs versus the West' kind of thing. It's very different from the United States where there's none of that. The United States still regards itself as at war with the Arab world, or Islam, or fundamentalism, or something of that sort. So the cultural issue is never really even tapped.

But when it comes to concrete political decisions, it would seem that Mediterranean Europe, which has been open, both in terms of migrations and culturally, to the Arab world, was not able to stop a war taking place in that part of the world.

Not only that, but in the case of Britain, participated rather more avidly than one would have liked. On the other hand, in the post-war period, the Italians and the French did try to broker a political, as opposed to a military, settlement. The Italians have been very active since the war on a negotiated political settlement, obviously not of the Gulf situation, but of the crux, which is the Palestinian issue. Now, they haven't been able to stand up obviously to the Americans for a number of reasons. Partly because their efforts are individual. They're not done in the name of Europe. I mean, the Council of Europe has taken very good positions, but they haven't acted together as a Community, and probably won't until after '92, if then. Individually, they are caught. On the one hand, they're pressured by the USA. On the other hand, they need oil from what are essentially conservative, reactionary Arab régimes who are very opposed to a change in the status quo. So their position is difficult. I'm really talking on a cultural level, where I think there is greater movement.

You've spoken a lot about the phenomenon of 'orientalism', a cultural phenomenon which basically represents a stereotypical attitude in Europe, and in the West generally, towards the Arab world.

Absolutely. It's really very powerful. You don't have to look in the jingoistic press. One thinks of the commentaries that one reads in *The Times* by, to mention names, Conor Cruise O'Brien who still talks about the Moslem family as a depraved family full of incest, and the Moslems and the Arabs as violent and depraved people, or books like *The Closed Circle* by David Pryce Jones, which could not be written about any other ethnic cultural group in the world today.

This is a sort of racism?

It's racism, it's xenophobia, it's a kind of paranoid, delusional fantasy.

And why has Europe needed this?

I'll tell you why. With regard to the Arabs Europe has always had Islam at its doorstep, so to speak. Islam, don't forget, is the only non-European culture that has never been completely vanquished. It is adjacent to and shares the monotheistic heritage with Judaism and Christianity. So, there is this constant friction. And unlike, say, the British in India, the problem has not been settled. The idea of the West, I would argue, comes largely from opposition to the Islamic and Arab world. I think it probably goes back in its root to theological issues. The prophet Mohammed, who saw himself as a continuer of the line of prophecy that begins with Abraham, Moses, Jesus, and concludes prophecy, is seen initially in the first polemics against Islam in the seventh and eighth century as an upstart, a terrifying emanation from exactly the world that produced Christianity and Judaism. So I think it's a unique case, and the sense of cultural contest is further enhanced by military, and you might say economic and political, contests where a tremendous amount of ignorance pervades, and people are not entitled, are not able therefore, to look at the concrete experience between Moslems and Europeans which is in reality much more complicated than sheer animosity. I mean, there is a tremendous dependence, for instance, in Europe on Islamic science, on the transmission of science and philosophy from the Greeks to the Moslems and back to the West.

I am struck as a philosopher by the crucial role played by Arab thinkers like Avicenna and Averroes, the Cordoba school, the Andalusian school, and so on.

Absolutely. And the idea of the university flourishes in the Arab world. The idea of a college, you know, *the collegium*, is, in fact, an Islamic idea.

We've had some rather dramatic examples, haven't we, of the confrontation between the European and Arab worlds in recent times? I'm not just thinking of the Gulf War, but also of controversies within Europe itself. We've had the Salman Rushdie affair, which raised all kinds of issues around universal rights versus the right to differ; and, in France, the famous controversy over the wearing of the veil by Moslem girls in secular schools. It's been a common argument that if Arab immigrants come to Europe, and have every right to do so having been colonised by Europeans for so many hundreds of years, they should leave behind them their cultural, religious differences and conform to this secular, universal space which is modern Europe.

I think there are universal principles of free speech to which Moslems as well as everyone else conform; and I think it's important that there is in the Arab world — I can't speak about *all* the Islamic world, Pakistan, Bangladesh, and so on — a very important struggle taking place today between the forces, broadly speaking, of what one would want to call *secularism*, to which I attach myself, and the forces that could be broadly described as *religious*. Now, fundamentalism is a frequent topic on the television, but I think it would be wrong to associate fundamentalism with everything that takes place in the Arab and Islamic world. I mean, there are different brands of that. There is a debate going on, and I think we are now at a point in the Arab world where the religious alternative has been shown to be a failure. You can be Moslem, but what does it mean to have Moslem economics, Moslem chemistry? In other words, there's a universal norm when it comes to running a modern state. But the question is, what of those people who represent another side of Islam, which is Islamic resistance to the West? On the West Bank in Gaza people consider themselves Islamic militants fighting Israeli occupation, because that's the last area of their lives that the Israelis have not been able to penetrate, as was the case in Algeria during the French occupation. So there are different kinds of Islam, there are different kinds of secularism. To come back to the Rushdie question, there were many Arab writers and intellectuals, including myself, who publicly supported Salman Rushdie's right to write whatever he chose, and that has to be underlined. But what we also drew attention to is the fact that there are many Moslem writers in the Arab world, in the Occupied Territories for example, who were put in jail by the Israelis as journalists and novelists for reasons of political expediency. For instance, speaking of banning books, on the West Bank today, because of Israeli law, you cannot buy and read Plato's *Republic*. Nor can you read Shakespeare's *Hamlet!* There is a proscribed list of many hundreds of books, prohibited by the Israelis for reasons nobody can understand. Now, where were the Western writers who stood up for Salman Rushdie — I'm glad they did, and I stood with them — when it came to the advocation of Palestinian freedom of expression on the West Bank and Gaza today? I don't know whether you know this, but the use of the word Palestine is a punishable offence. If you use the word Palestine you can be put in jail for six months. So what about a single standard for all these things? Why hypocritically use this? We're in the same fight with you. We want also to fight against that kind of thing, but let us fight on *all* fronts.

There's been much talk in recent times about creating a new European order, a federal Europe of regions or nations, and there's been talk about creating a new world information order — I'm thinking especially of the UNESCO Report sponsored by the late Sean MacBride. Are you suggesting we should interpret this as a struggle to create a secular universal order?

I'm not sure I know. I'm not in favour of an abstract universalism, because it's usually the universalism of whoever happens to be most powerful. If you look around today, the language of universalism is proclaimed by the United States, which is the super-power — one would like to think it's the last superpower. Without wishing to preach to the converted, it does seem to me that Ireland could play an important role in all of this, because Ireland has a colonial past. Although European, it is different from Europe, noticeably from continental Europe, and it would seem to me that instead of the submergence of various European countries like Ireland into the general European personality, highlighting the differences would be very important for dealing precisely with other parts of the colonial world. For instance, it seems to me that Ireland has a very special role to play, not only in Palestine, by virtue of the divisions in this country, but also in South Africa. Highlighting differences and allowing that to engage Europe's others in a kind of exchange could be very important in breaking down the idea of the world in great cultural camps, which in the end become armed camps. No, I have nothing but suspicion for the kind of universalism that is sometimes talked about.

But would you have some hope that we can in the Western world, and in Europe in particular, overcome the traditional antagonism between 'them' and 'us'? Do you see the possibility of some kind of solidarity being created between those in Europe struggling for basic liberties and rights, and those within the Arab world who are doing exactly the same thing?

Yes, I think that is the hope, precisely that. It *is* a common struggle. But even more important than that, what struck me the most about the war and about the behaviour of the Iraqis and even the response of Palestinians, was that this was a war of decrepit or diseased nationalism. I think the great problem is the whole issue of national identity, or what I would call the *politics of identity* — the feeling that everything you do has to be either legitimated by, or has to pass through the filter of, your national identity, which in most instances is a complete fiction, as we all know. I mean, an identity that says all Arabs are homogeneously the same and against all Westerners who are all the same. There are many Westerners, there are many Arabs. I think the principal role of the intellectual at this point is to break up these large, national, cultural, trans-cultural identities.

Whether it is pan-Arab nationalism or Euro-nationalism?

Yes. I mean, there is an Arab people, there is an Arab nation. It doesn't need defence, we know that. But what we need is to reclaim it from the rhetoric of nationalism which has been hijacked by regimes in the Arab world. You tell me what the Saudi Arabian regime, government, or the Syrian government, or the Egyptian government has to do with Arab nationalism. I tell you, zero, nothing. They are in the business of *using* Arab nationalism. Or take their defence of Palestine. They have betrayed the Intifada, they do nothing for it. And they use the notion, not only of a national identity but of a beleaguered national identity which produces the national security state, the repressive apparatus, the secret police, the army, as an instrument of repression. The same in Israel. The same idea, it's everywhere. The same in the United States. Can anyone persuade me that what the United States was fighting in the Gulf was an aggression that threatened the United States? Does security enter into it? That's total, absolute, complete nonsense. But the resurgent American identity needed and used the security issue. What about the real struggle for freedoms? Human freedoms which are central — freedom of expression, freedom of assembly, of opinion, and so on. And then, the political freedoms. Where today, for example, we know it's a scandal in South Africa that a vast majority of the inhabitants are not allowed the right to vote. But also the States of Europe and the United States who underwrite, subsidise, the denial of democratic freedoms for an entire nation, the Palestinians. I mean, that's a scandal also. But you have to get beyond the politics of identity to be able to talk about these things.

Are you then advocating a movement beyond the rival nationalisms of the Arab world on the one hand, and of Europe on the other hand? And do you see a danger of a relapse into nationalisms in Europe that would again be a mirror image for a similar occurrence in the Arab world?

I think that's obviously the great trap. What I would prefer to see is a Europe that is more aware, for example, of its colonial history. In other words, not to simply say, well, we've superseded that, we're something else now. Your history as Europeans is also a colonial history; and North Africa, for example, has to be dealt with as a fact that informs your present behaviour and informs your relationship with these former colonised cultures.

Do you mean acknowledging also the immigrants who are a part of us?

There has to be an understanding, finally, that there is no political or national grouping that is homogeneous. Everything we are talking about is mixed, we deal in a world of interdependent, mongrelised societies. They are hybrids, they are impure.

Which is a strength and a virtue.

To me it's a virtue. What you're beginning to see now is a rhetoric of purification. I'm talking about the Far Right, let's say, in France, Le Pen. The idea that Europe is for the Europeans, you're beginning to hear it now. On one level, of course, it's fighting off the United States, and also Japan. Look at the rhetoric of Japan-bashing. The fundamental question is education. Most systems of education today, I believe, are still nationalist, that is to say, they promote the authority of the national identity in an idealised way and suggest that it is incapable of any criticism, it is incapable of any fault, it is virtue incarnate. There is nothing that lays the seed of conflict in the future more than what we educate our children and students in the universities to believe about ourselves.

Would you advocate multi-culturalism, that we should read the texts of other traditions as well as the great Western texts?

I think so. Take America, for example. There has been a tremendous debate recently about the figure of Columbus. I mean, we're in 1992, which is the five hundredth anniversary of the discovery of the United States by Columbus. The figure of Columbus itself is a highly controversial one, but he has been domesticated, sanitised into this wonderful hero who discovered America, whereas, in fact, he was a slave trader, he was a colonial conqueror, he was very much in the tradition of the *conquistador*. Now, which is better, to prettify and sanitise or to admit the truth? And there is this ridiculous idea that if you don't do this inventing of tradition, which will produce a hero figure, who's basically a conqueror — you threaten the fabric of society. I say just the opposite — the fabric of society, particularly American society, but it's also true of Europe, contains many different elements, and one has to recognise them. I think children are perfectly capable of understanding that. It's the adults who don't want to understand that for base reasons.

PAUL RICOEUR

Universality and the Power of Difference

Paul Ricoeur: Europe has produced a series of cultural identities, which brought with themselves their self-criticism, and I think that this is unique. Even Christianity encompassed its own critique.

Richard Kearney: And how would you see that critique operating? In forms of Reformation and Renaissance?
Yes, but not only in the plurality of theologies, but also in some repressed Churches, repressed cultural spiritualities. Plurality is within Europe itself. Europe has had different kinds of Renaissance, we speak now of Carthaginian Renaissance, twelfth century Renaissance, Italian and French Renaissance, fifteenth century, and so on. The Enlightenment was another expression of that; and it is important that in the dialogue with other cultures we keep this element of self-criticism, which I think is the only specificity of Europe along with, of course, the enhancement of science.

What you say about Europe and our ability to criticise ourselves is one side of our heritage, and a good side, but isn't there another positive side — the affirmation of a certain universality in our philosophy?
Our specificity also is that we have had to intertwine several heritages — Jewish-Christian, Greek-Roman, then the Barbarian cultures which were encompassed within the Roman Empire, the heritage within Christianity of the Reformation, this rock of Renaissance Enlightenment, and also the three nineteenth-century components of this heritage, *nationalism, socialism,* and *romanticism...*

PAUL RICOEUR is a French philosopher
who has held Chairs at the Universities of
Paris and Chicago. His books include
History and Truth, *The Rule of Metaphor*,
Time and Narrative, *Hermeneutics and the
Human Sciences*, *The Conflict of
Interpretations* and *Self as Other*.

And those three put into question a certain universality of Europe by affirming particularities ...

Yes, it means that the kind of universality that Europe represents contains within itself a plurality of cultures, which have been merged and intertwined, and which provide a certain fragility, an ability to disclaim and question itself.

This of course opens the question, doesn't it, of how we in Europe relate not just to the differences within our borders and boundaries, but also how we relate to the differences of other non-European continents and countries; and how the universalist project of Europe can engage in dialogue with their differences, their nationalisms, their fundamentalisms? I mean, can we preach to others if we haven't sorted out our own problems of national identity?

I think we must be very cautious here in Europe when we speak of fundamentalism, because it is immediately a pejorative word, and this prevents good analysis. We have to look at the phenomenon because there are several kinds of fundamentalism. We put one word above a multiplicity of events. But there is, for instance, a difference between a return to a culture close to the practice of the people and a fundamentalism imposed from above.

Well, if we take the example of the Baltic States in Europe, do you have a sympathy with what their nationalist claims for sovereignty and autonomy are trying to achieve?

I must say that I am surprised by the extent of the phenomenon, but also the extremist dimension, because in all my own philosophical culture, I had underestimated the capacity of language to reorganise a culture and to unify it. And secondly, I had also underestimated the fragility of each identity which feels threatened by the other. People must be very unsure to feel threatened by the otherness of the other. I did not realise that people are so unsure when they claim so emphatically to be what they are.

Wouldn't you agree that there are very good historical reasons for this insecurity, not only in the Baltic States, but also in Yugoslavia, in Czechoslovakia, or in Northern Ireland — hence the need to attach themselves to a separatist national identity?

But there is also the fact that there is no political distribution of borders which is adequate to the distribution of languages and cultures, so there is no political solution at the level of the Nation State. This is the real irritator of the nineteenth century, this dream of a perfect equation between a State and a Nation.

That clearly has failed.

Yes, that has failed. So, we have to look for something else.

Well, we are looking. It is extremely relevant at the moment, where somebody like Jacques Delors, the President of the Community, is talking about the necessity to go beyond the limitations of the Nation State (while preserving it as an intermediary model) to a trans-national federation of States on the one hand, and a devolution of power from the Nation State to regions on the other hand — to regions that would be more self-governing, that would encourage the practice of local democracy, of participatory democracy. Do you think that might work?

Yes, but there is a political problem — what is better? Is it a federalism, a confederation of regions, or of nations and so on? I don't know the solution because it is something without a precedent. Modern history has been made by Nation States. And you also have countries like France which have a strong identity as a Nation State; there is also difference of size, because we have five or six Nation States in Europe which are of middle size in comparison to China, but we have micro-nations which cannot become micro-states in the same way as national states have succeeded.

Well, it may well be unprecedented in Europe, but one could argue that it's not unprecedented in what some call the 'other Europe' of Canada and the United States, where they did have a model of federation, and indeed a certain amount of local autonomy in government at the level of the town halls, particularly at the beginning of the American Revolution.

But, in a sense, the United States is an opposite case because it is a melting pot of immigrants.

But surely we've also got an opportunity to enter into a new relationship with the immigrants from those countries we went and colonised for two or three hundred years.

The United States has solved the problem with a unit of language, English, to a certain extent. We have an opposite problem, we have to deal with a multiplicity of languages, I don't know how many languages, maybe thirty or forty languages competing....

I'd like to bring in the question of sovereignty here. At the moment we're agreeing to pool sovereignty in Europe. The notion of sovereignty, if I'm not mistaken, actually goes back to the idea, first of all, that God is the universal sovereign, later replaced by the King as sovereign, as the centre of one indivisible power. Then, with the replacement of monarchy by republics, with the French Revolution, for example, the Nation State became sovereign.

In modern republics, the origin of sovereignty is in the people, but now we recognise that we have many peoples. And many peoples means many centres of sovereignty — we have to deal with that.

Wasn't one of the problems of the French Revolution the definition of sovereignty as one and indivisible? That creates problems when you export the Revolution to other countries or continents.

Take the Corsican people who are also a member of the French people. Here we have two meanings of the word *people*. On the one hand, 'people' means to be a citizen in a state, so it's not a cultural concept, it's not a ethnic concept. But, on the other hand, Corsica *is* a people in an ethnic sense — within the French people which is not an ethnic concept. So, we are fighting with two concepts of people, and I think it's a good example of what is happening throughout Europe now.

Does this mean two different kinds of membership — ethnic membership and civic membership?

Yes, because the notion of 'people' according to the French Constitution is not ethnic. Its citizenship is defined by the fact that somebody is born on the territory of France. For example, the son or daughter of an immigrant is French because he or she was born on this territory. So, the rule of membership has nothing to do with ethnic origin. This is why it was impossible to define Corsican people, because then we had to rely on criteria other than citizenship, on ethnic criteria, and who, to whom are we to apply these criteria?

You're into the very dangerous area of racism.

And then in fact we inject the criteria of citizenship to moderate the excess of the ethnic criteria.

To enlarge the discussion somewhat, could one not say that there are in fact several Europes?
The German thinker, Karl Jaspers, used to say that Europe extends from San Francisco to Vladivostok. This raises the issue of the cultural expansion of Europe.

Perhaps the ultimate solution, if one is to be found, is not to be found within the limits of Europe. Maybe we need to extend those limits and go further to what some people have called a world republic, a cosmopolitan state which can harbour differences yet bind all peoples and all continents together?
Even in political terms, maybe it's impossible to solve the problem of the unification of Europe without solving the problem of some international institution which would provide the proper framework.

This Utopian vision of a world republic, or a European republic, is one that goes back to the Enlightenment, to Kant and Montesquieu ...
We need now a plurality of Utopias, Utopias of different kinds. Surely, a basic Utopia is a world economy which is not ruled by efficiency, by productivity, but based on needs. Maybe this will be the problem for the next century — how to move from an economy ruled by the laws of the market to a universal economy based on the real needs of people. This is Utopia. We are now at the stage where the market is winning and provides the only source of productivity, but this productivity is not shared, because the success of productivity increases inequality. We'll have to solve it. Secondly, we have political Utopia. What kind of institution have we to invent at the level of the world community, at the level of Europe, and the level of political entities around the Pacific Ocean, and so on? So we're talking about a hierarchy of sovereignties. This will be another problem.

If we can take a step back from the immediate political implications of this problem and say a little about the cultural and philosophical presuppositions of this discussion.

I would like to centre the discussion about the role of *memory* in this context. Because, on the one hand, memory is a burden; if we keep repeating the story of wars won or lost, we keep reinforcing the old hostilities. Take the different States of Europe. In fact, we cannot find a pair who weren't at war at one time or another. The French and the British, the Poles and the Germans, and so on. So, there is a memory which is a prison, which is regressive. But, on the other hand, we cannot do without the cultivation of the memory of our cultural achievements, and also of our sufferings. This brings me to the second element. We need a memory of the second order which is based on forgiving. And we cannot forgive if we have forgotten. So, in fact we have to *cross* our memories, to *exchange* our memories with each other to the point that, for example, the crimes of the Germans become part of our own memory. Sharing the memory of cruelty of my neighbour is a part of this political dimension of forgiving. We have some examples. When the German Chancellor went to Warsaw and knelt down and asked for pardon, I think that was very important for Europe. Because, while we have to get rid of the memory of wars, of victory, and so on, we must keep the memory of the scars. Then we can proceed to this exchange of memories, to this mutual forgiveness.

It's an unusual idea.
I don't see how we can solve Europe's problems only in terms of a Common Market or a political institution. We need these, of course. We need the extension of a free market which would be the basis of the unification for Europe and also a relationship between Europe and the rest of the world, the invention of new institutions to solve the problem of the multiplicity of Nation States. But there is a spiritual problem underlying both the economic problem of a Common Market and the political problem of new institutions which cannot be the same as American ones.

And what would the role of narrative — one of the key concepts in your philosophy — be in relation to this cultural crisis that we are facing in Europe today? I mean narrative as story-telling, as remembrance or as projection.

I would say three things concerning the role of narrative. First you have the narration of founding events, because most cultures have some original happening or act which gives some basis of unity to the diversity within the culture. Hence the need to commemorate founding events.

Such as the French Revolution, the Soviet Revolution, 1916 in Ireland?
Yes. We have to keep that because we have to retain some claims, some convictions that are rooted in these founding events. Secondly, I would say that one of the resources of the theory of narrativity is that now we know that we may tell *different* stories about ourselves. So, we have to learn how to vary the stories that we are telling about ourselves. And thirdly, we have to enter this process of exchange, which the German philosophers called *Auseinandersetzung*. We are caught in the stories of the others, so we are protagonists in the stories we are told by others, and we have to assume for ourselves the stories that the others tell about us, which have their own founding events, their own intrigues, their own plots.

So the crossing of memories involves the crossing of stories. But is there any sense in which in Europe today we can tell each other the same story, a common universal European story? Is there anything to bind us together?
I would say that this concept of universality may be used in different contexts. On the one hand, you may speak of universal rules of discourse — what Habermas says about rules of discussion, let us say the logic and ethics of argumentation. This is one level of universality, but it is too formal to be operative. Secondly, you have a universalist claim within our own culture. For example, we may claim that some rights to free speech are universal, in spite of the fact that for the time being they cannot be included within other cultures. But it's a claim, it remains a claim, as long as it is not recognised by the others. So we bring to the discussion claims of universality — not only procedures of universality but claims of universality. And thirdly, I would say that you have a kind of eschatological universalism — the universal as an ultimate project or goal as in Kant's *Essay on Perpetual Peace*, and so on.

The project of some kind of universal republic.

The project of universality is central to the whole debate about human rights. Take the example of the mutilation of women. I am sure that we are right to say that there is something universal in our assertion that women have a right to pleasure, to physical integrity and so on, even if it is not recognised. But we have to bring that into the discussion. It's only the discussion which may finally convince the other that it's universal, because a claim, as long as it is not recognised by the other, remains a claim.

VÁCLAV HAVEL is one of Europe's foremost living playwrights and essayists. Sentenced to four and a half years' hard labour in his native Czechoslovakia for his involvement in the 'Charter 77' human rights movement, Havel went on to become President of his country in 1989. His plays include *Memorandum, Largo Desolato, Temptation* and *Slum Clearance*. His prose collections include *Living in Truth* and *Letters to Olga*.

VÁCLAV HAVEL

Plays and Politics

Václav Havel: Politicians deceive people when they offer them a complete recipe for human happiness, and maintain that only their political decisions and measures can make humans happy. Man is not only an object of political measures. Man is something more. Politics can offer only a limited number of things. It can provide and develop conditions under which people can lead a more dignified life; it can guarantee certain liberties. However it cannot guarantee an earthly paradise; it cannot promise people will be happy without having to move hand or foot. This is the border, the threshold where the ideal ends and utopia begins. Taking into account today's changes, our society should and must have certain ideals but cannot and must not substitute another utopia for the communist one.

Richard Kearney: We are talking about positive and negative ideas — about ideals and visions. In Czechoslovakia, the intellectual has had an important role. When one looks back at your history, you had men of ideas who were national heros, for example Comenius, the educator; and Jan Hus, the humanist theologian; and then in the twentieth century your first president, Tomas Masaryk, was a philosopher — as was also Jan Patoçka, one of the founder members of Charter 77 (in which you also played a very central role). In one of your essays 'Six asides on culture', you mention Patoçka and say it's not an accident that this 'victim in the struggle for civil and human rights' in your country was also a thinker. What is this special Czechoslovak tradition of the intellectual? And do you think it an accident that the Czechoslovak people have now chosen as President, someone like you who is a leading writer and intellectual?

In my case, more than one reason led to my election. It is true, however, that intellectuals — writers, philosophers — have traditionally played a more significant and important role in both

Czech and Slovak public life than they have played in other countries. Our nation, our society, has constantly been oppressed and endangered, its political rights always restricted — during the Austro-Hungarian Empire as well as in the communist era. In these situations, in which civil and political or national rights are restricted, chances that professional politicians will mature are limited and intellectuals naturally take over. Who else should take over? Telling the truth under oppression is itself a political phenomenon and the tellers automatically become public figures. It was mostly intellectuals who represented the outspoken opposition in the communist era. This is why those intellectuals who had been telling the truth about the system aloud for many years were lately given public offices. They were not representatives of professional politicians and opposition parties. There are many people like me in the government and in the parliament. Of course, following the stabilisation of democracy, a new generation of professional politicians will come — and is already coming — into the political and public life of our country. The public role of intellectuals is likely to diminish. They will play the role of a mirror which reflects public life but they will not be the main actors.

You were first and foremost a playwright, working in the theatre; and the theatre played quite a central role in the Velvet Revolution in your country in 1989. You mentioned in one of your writings that each new work of theatre weakened the repressive regime. What is there about theatre in the Czech situation that proved so subversive and so revolutionary?

This question has several aspects. Firstly, to follow up what I was saying earlier: art, culture and intellectuals play an increasingly political role in oppressive conditions. This is what happened in our country in the sixties and — subject to some changes — in the seventies and eighties. Theatres were centres of resistance, even if the resistance was limited because all theatres were marked by censorship. However, theatres were spiritual focal points, enclaves in which certain liberties flourished, most obviously in the sixties. Ever since the National Revival in the beginning of the nineteenth century, when performances in the Czech language had been helping to support national self-realisation, theatres have played an important role in our lives. Secondly, theatres played an important role in our revolution.

They supported the rioting students immediately after the massacre. Scheduled performances were cancelled and theatres became public places where discussions were taking place and where, at a certain stage, the revolution was actually happening. The third aspect is a more general and metaphysical: the theatrical, dramatic dimension of those changes in our country. The dramatic structure was here: acts, peripetia, crises etc. The features of various dramatic genres were here too: tragedy, comedy, absurd theatre, farce and (very markedly) a fairy-tale. The events had their actors. Singers also played key roles at mass meetings and manifestations. Changes in our country had theatrical and dramatic dimensions.

You have written that you are against '-isms' and ideologies and for the development of an individual moral conscience. But how does one develop an individual moral conscience that remains open to some notion of a common social good and does not return to the old classical liberalism of each-person-for-him-or-herself? What is the moral basis or motivation behind this kind of conscience?

The era of ideologies seems to have come to an end. I think that we are entering an era of thinking now. Ideological systems and doctrines either wore out and failed like Marxism or became a danger, a threat. The alternative is a future rehabilitation of the human subject — conscience and thought as such: the rehabilitation of thinking which originates in the human subject and is not transmissible by some system of precepts or dogmas. Regarding the connection with classical liberalism: the rehabilitation of the subject includes something which has been neglected in the nineteenth century. The era of liberalism was in love with science and technology and in this era the conception of man as a sovereign master of the world was born. When I speak about the rehabilitation of the subject or about an 'existential revolution', I really mean something more: the renaissance or revival of human responsibilities, of a relation between man and something mysterious which is more than man, some metaphysical assurance. When I speak of the re-establishment of the human subject, I do not have in mind 'Man' at the top of an existential pyramid, man who has no master and therefore can do as he pleases.

In your 'Open letter to President Husak' in 1975, you write about an order without history, without culture and without morality — an order of tyranny and fear that has been imposed on your society. And you say to President Husak: 'How profound a moral impotence will the nation suffer tomorrow following the castration of its culture today?' Seventeen years later you are now sitting where President Husak once sat, here in Prague Castle. Do you feel that there has been some profound damage done to your nation during the post-war period of oppression; and if so, how does one repair it? How do you bring back a sense of culture, a sense of morality?

First of all, let me say that when President Husak was sitting here, the social circumstances were totally different from those of today. I am not a representative of an authoritative, totalitarian regime. In my office, I have been trying with the help of others to rebuild Czechoslovak democracy. Of course I feel that my duty is to keep stressing certain moral values — to lay the emphasis on the spiritual dimension of human life and to face the danger of commercialisation which comes hand in hand with the market economy: to emphasise constantly that consumer society alone cannot secure human happiness and the future of humankind. This has always been and still is my opinion.

You have spoken about the possibility of a partyless politics, and even an 'anti-political politics'. But today you as President have a critical and central role in politics. How is it possible to reconcile your role as writer — where you say 'the primary function is to live within truth' — and your political function as leader of the land? Is it possible to combine the two? Or would you like, as soon as possible, to do yourself out of a job?

I was given this job by fate. As long as I hold this office, I must try to work in harmony with myself, to live up to and act according to my convictions. I cannot put aside my identity and become somebody else in the course of my term as president. Even today I fight a battle against party dictatorship. Of course I do not oppose the existence of political parties. That would be nonsense. Pluralistic democracy cannot exist without the existence of political parties. I am against the dictatorship of a party, against the secret power of party secretariats, against the type of situation in which deputies have more duties to bureaucracies and secretariats than to the people who voted for them. I keep fighting unsuccessfully for a different election system in our country. I think that the personal guarantee must be stressed. Party anonymity leads to collective irresponsibility.

Mikhail Gorbachev said recently that the revolutionary changes in Eastern Europe and in the Soviet Union could not have taken place if it was not for the Pope. Do you think that religion and religious sensibility has played a positive role in these changes? After all when you were elected you quoted Masaryk's famous phrase, 'Jesus not Caesar'.

The renaissance of faith has played a certain role in recent changes as well as the fact that it was Karol Wojtyla who became Pope. However, I do not think this was the chief and single reason for those big changes in our part of the world. The totalitarian system wore out, rotted from within. People were unable to bear the continuous pressure of the system any more, rioting and resistance started. The system was leading to crises in every aspect of our society. I do not think that the Pope or Gorbachev are the sole figures responsible for all these changes. Indeed Gorbachev played a very important role in the process and had he not become the General Secretary of the Communist Party in the Soviet Union, the changes would probably have come later and would have been different, but they were bound to come sooner or later. Perestroika obviously played a key role but the changes did not come as a result of perestroika alone. They were due to more than any one reason.

In Europe at the moment — particularly the ex-Soviet block and Yugoslavia — there seems to be a slide or degeneration into separatist nationalist movements. Is there a danger that in Czechoslovakia today a similar movement towards separatist nationalism could destroy the possibility of a genuine Federation?

I do not know how the constitutional law will develop in our country. I do not even know if this country is going to be divided into two independent states, although I don't think it is likely. Many nations, and also the Slovak nation, are going through a certain process of emancipation. But I do not think that what has happened in some parts of the former Soviet Union or in Yugoslavia will happen here. There was never a war between Czechs and Slovaks, they have never fought against each other, there was never a time when one of them conquered the other nation. I cannot see why our country should be afflicted with such dramatic and violent conflict.

Finally a question about Europe. You once spoke about the possibility of a European Federation, based on the Council of Europe, that would include the Middle or Eastern European countries. What is your vision for Europe, and for Czechoslovakia's role in Europe, in the years to come?

I cannot know exactly what course the European integration process will take. It depends on many people, governments, parliaments, geopolitical interests etc. It is not something which I myself could plan. However, I have said publicly before that the idea of a united, confederate Europe is a good idea, that this is the path Europe should take and does take. It is difficult to say which institution will become the leading one. There are many international organisations in Europe: the Helsinki Process, the Council of Europe, the EC, NATO etc. At this moment, it is difficult to tell what role each of them will play in the future or how these existing multinational organisations will be linked. The Helsinki Process could give a basic frame to the continuing integration, the Council of Europe could get the upper hand in the field of political culture and the setting of legal standards, while the EC remains the driving force of economic and political unification. I suppose that they will all be gradually linked closer together and Europe will hopefully become a more united continent, based on a unity of diversity.

H.E. MARY ROBINSON

A Question of Law:
The European Legacy

Richard Kearney: *What contribution has Europe made to the development of modern law?*

Mary Robinson: Modern Europe has been very creative and very innovative in developing frameworks of law affecting different countries. For example, in the Fifties, a number of countries came together and subscribed to the European Convention for the Protection of Human Rights and Fundamental Freedoms, and that was part of the Council of Europe organisation, which is thriving today and indeed reaching out to the new and emerging states in Eastern Europe. It has a very good framework for protecting individual rights, enforced through the Commission and Court of Human Rights sitting in Strasbourg. It also has a Council of Europe which brings out broad guidance laws and advisory reports on a wide number of areas — they're not binding internally in the laws of the Member States, but they can have a very significant influence in the area of the environment, consumer protection, or whatever.

This European Convention of Human Rights covers most of the European countries, doesn't it — it's larger than the EC twelve member States?

That's right. It includes more than twenty-five countries, and the number is increasing as Eastern European countries apply. The countries who join commit themselves in a very interesting way to the compulsory jurisdiction of the Commission and Court of Human Rights. It means that either another Member State can bring an action before the Commission and Court, as indeed Ireland did against the United Kingdom for torture and ill-treatment of those held in custody in Northern Ireland, and that went

MARY ROBINSON is President of Ireland and is the first woman to hold this office. She held a Chair of Law at Trinity College Dublin for many years and was a member of the International Jurists. She is an expert on European law.

to the Commission and ultimately to the Court, which found that there had been ill-treatment, which didn't amount to full torture but was in breach of the Convention. It's also possible for individuals to bring a case against their own government; and there have been a number of cases against Ireland, a number of cases against most of the European countries. Interestingly, Sweden has had a very large number of cases brought against it, although you might think that Sweden had a good system of protecting human rights. Often, it's when the system is quite sophisticated that citizens are more aware of their rights and can bring cases before the Commission and the Court.

This is a question of citizens bringing a case against their own member State by appealing to a broader European Convention.

Yes, and there is a common-sense procedural provision that before you bring a case to Strasbourg, you should have exhausted the possibilities of going before your own Court, exhausted your domestic remedies. So, it may be that you'd have a case going, for example, in Ireland, the High Court and Supreme Court, and then go to Strasbourg. But if you don't have a domestic remedy, if there isn't any right you can enforce in your national Court, you may be able to go to Strasbourg straight away. The value of this is very well perceived now by the emerging Eastern European countries, and I would suppose that when the Commonwealth of new states that is replacing the Soviet Union gets under way, they will either devise a similar mechanism, or they will wish to subscribe to the existing procedure that is there — the framework which has now a very important body of jurisprudence, of law that has been built up, very experienced judges, and a whole system that is respected and is very innovative for these countries which are forgoing their sovereignty in the area of human rights. It's a very important resource. That's one area where I think Europe has been innovative.

If the European Convention of Human Rights is a civil law tradition, how does it operate in a common law tradition like England or Ireland?

Well, it was drafted by the governments who were there in the Fifties to subscribe to it, including the Irish government. Sean MacBride, for example, played a significant role in the drafting of the European Convention. The Commission, which is the first body to assess a possible case, and then the Court, have applied a case by case approach, but they've also been influenced by the civil law approach of many of the countries, where the text is very important and the way in which the text is interpreted is more purposive, it looks more to the objective of the text than would be the case in the more pragmatic common law approach. Certainly as a lawyer in the past who pleaded before the Commission and Court of Human Rights, I was conscious that it wasn't the same as going before an Irish court, that there was this influence of the civil law system. That's also true in the European Community structure, which is another great innovation of Europe.

But how is a civil law tradition to be applied to legal traditions like ours? I think that the blending of the civil law and our own common law approaches is even more interesting and noticeable in what I would say is a tighter legal framework of the European Community. We're now talking about the twelve member States, including Ireland, who have subscribed to treaties originally, but that has begun to develop into a European Community constitution, and the Court in Luxembourg is working in a kind of judicial harmony with national courts, because a lot of the cases, particularly cases that affect individual rights under Community Law, are referred by a national court. The national court will have initially probably decided under its own national approach to interpreting. The matter is then referred to the Court in Luxembourg which may, looking at the particular measure in the particular European context, give a different interpretation. I can give you a good example of that from the Irish situation. An equal pay claim was brought by a significant number of women workers in Bord Telecom, who had no man doing exactly what they were doing (making telephone components), so they compared themselves with a man on their shop-floor, who was not doing the *same* work, but they claimed he was doing *like* work. And this went before the Equality Officer, who under Irish legislation implementing European Directives on equal pay, provided a means of assessing the work, and concluded that these women were doing work of *higher* value, of superior value to the man, and therefore under Irish law that this was not like work, and the case couldn't succeed. The Labour Court, before whom the case was appealed, also said under Irish law they could not succeed in their claim because it was not *like* work.

So their claim for equal pay couldn't succeed even though they were getting less pay for superior work.

Yes. And the matter was then appealed to the High Court, and the High Court judge in a very careful judgement said that he felt that the Equality Officer and Labour Court were correct under strictly Irish canons of interpretation, but he doubted whether this was compatible with the European approach. So he took the appropriate course of making a reference to the Luxembourg Court, the Court of the European Communities, and that Court, because it adopted a completely different approach, looked at the purpose of the guarantee in Article 119 of the European Treaty, and the purpose of the relevant Directive, and said that if the work was of higher value, it was of at least equal value. In order to enforce equality and not have gaps in the enforcement, there would be an entitlement to equal pay. The matter then went back to the Irish High Court, which had made the reference. The judge very carefully explained why he now reached a different conclusion, because the European Court had interpreted in a different way and that was binding on him, and he referred it back to the Labour Court and said it's also binding on the Labour Court, and they must now apply that law. So, not only does the Court in Luxembourg adopt a different approach in important ways to the interpretation of the Treaty and of Directives or Regulations at Community level, but this directly influences the national courts, including the Irish courts. It's very enriching, it's a way of ensuring a more rounded guarantee of rights for the individual, rights that are given directly by virtue of European Law.

Have there been instances of the European written Constitution actually being applied in a country like Great Britain, with its common law tradition and no written constitution, in a way that has actually benefited that tradition?

I think it has been even more striking in the United Kingdom, which doesn't have a written constitution. Our Courts, our High Court and Supreme Court, are accustomed to a constitutional law which is closer to the European Community law. Interpreting the Constitution and if necessary setting aside Irish legislation, declaring it null and void, if it infringes the Constitution, is closer to enforcing Community rights, and if necessary setting aside national law which is in conflict with the Community law, because the Community law takes precedence, is supreme, over national law which is in conflict with it. This has been a very real challenge to the English courts, and there is now quite a literature about the impact of the European Community Treaties on British law, that it has in fact brought in, in the areas where it applies, a written constitution through the European back-door. It has also meant that the House of Lords, for example, is now applying European law in accordance with this purposive approach and will if necessary be quite inventive in writing in a phrase to ensure that the purpose of the law is enforced. There is a judicial and legal excitement about that. There's a lot of writing about it, a lot of analysis of the effects of it.

So there isn't that sense of the British establishment, whatever about the British people, holding out against Europe for national reasons as in the run-up to Maastricht. In law, it seems to have worked in a very co-operative manner.

In law it has worked in a co-operative manner because the binding nature of the law is very clear, and it has been accepted and applied by the judges and courts. It's interesting to note that of the twelve member States of the European Community, Ireland is the closest to the United States — because Ireland has, first of all, an English-speaking background, it has the common law and yet (unlike Britain but like the US) it also has a written constitution. I think that has helped our judges and courts, and indeed our lawyers, to have an easier familiarity with the impact of European Community law, and its binding effect — the fact that it can at times supersede and have a direct applicability, which means that any conflicting national law has to be either set aside or declared null and void by the courts. The process of digestion, if I can put it that way, of Community law into Ireland is the closest to a process of digestion that would occur if the United States was a member of the Community. This, I think, has been a factor that has interested American lawyers who have studied European law. You have to look at it at the two levels. If you want to study European Community law you can't just do it at the level of what happens in Brussels. You must also take at least one Member State and see how that law has been applied, how it is enforced either directly or through the national enforcement of local courts.

But are there other areas outside of law, or outside of inter-governmental contact and exchange, where we stand to benefit?

Yes, very much so. There was a tendency to think that the European framework was first of all very legalistic — Regulations and Directives coming out of Brussels and being enforced by the national courts. I think in recent years there has been a realisation that there must also be a possibility of different groups using the wider European framework, but using it in a way that penetrates right down to the local level. And I've been glad to see that happening more and more. For example, the European Community has been providing supports for the disabled in our society, mentally or physically disabled. There are various ways in which voluntary bodies and State bodies working with the disabled can link into the European level. Earlier this year, I opened a conference of Eureka, a European colloquium on Culture and the Disabled which involved a number of European countries. That is assisted by, and stimulated by, some funding at the European Community level, but really the energy comes from linkages, local voluntary linkages, using that umbrella framework.

This networking that you're describing operates at a small level, and somebody might object that the movement in Europe at the moment is towards the centre, that we're now seeing a situation where wealth and resources and power are being gathered into Brussels, and that really these sorts of peripheral activities are all very good, but they won't change anything.

Well, I think that is one potential danger in the development of Europe. It's also a possible way of describing national communities at the moment, these energies at local level, that self-development and voluntary organisations are growing, notwithstanding quite a lot of centralisation of power and resources. I think there is a very strong movement at European level for more regional and local taking of decisions. There is the concept of subsidiarity, that decisions should be taken at the optimum level, and the optimum level is the lowest level at which that decision can be well taken. Again, hopefully this may affect the national systems of the European countries as well.

There's a new committee of regions that's just been set up and approved in the Maastricht Treaty.

Yes, I think the way in which this can be encouraged is by having a networking of the more local self-development and community groups which are substantially voluntary. Most of these have very few full-time paid workers. They may have one or two facilitators, and the rest of the group are either voluntary or part-time workers.

But not powerless. You would see this power moving from the ground up as being an essential movement.

I think it certainly can be reinforced through all sorts of linkages. It can be fostered and encouraged by seeing that in other countries a similar development is taking place. There is a lot of energy and local knowledge there. There is a lot of awareness of how an integrated approach to rural development can grow from the bottom up, and I would certainly like to see that developing with the learning experience of a Europe of cultural diversity, and a Europe of social diversity.

As we move towards European unity, it could be said that we're going to expose ourselves to the danger of cultural uniformity — a sort of lowest-common-denominator culture. Would you hold out any hope that it is possible to preserve and foster cultural diversity within this new context?

Well, again, looking at the Irish experience, since we joined in 1973, our participation in Europe has been very good psychologically. It's hard to define precisely what is meant by that, but it has been good for Ireland to be one among, first of all nine, then ten when Greece joined, and now twelve, with the joining of Spain and Portugal. Twelve Member States. We have things in common and we have our differences. When Ireland has the Presidency, as it has had for six-month periods, those representatives of governments come to Dublin, or come to parts of Ireland, for discussions, and Irish Ministers and the Taoiseach participate at the European level. That, I think, has reinforced our sense of nationhood, our psychological sense of identity. It has led to a maturing of relations between Ireland and Britain.

We are less under the shadow of Big Brother. We are less dictated to by British farm policy, and cheap food policy, than we were in the past.

And we also discover we have many common interests with Britain. The same language, for instance, to state the most obvious.

Exactly. And quite often common approaches which are affected by legal approaches, what we were talking about earlier, our shared approach of common law systems. This, I believe, has also given us a sense that in the Europe of twelve member States now linking with the EFTA countries, the *cultural* background of those countries is extremely important; and looked at in that perspective, Irish culture comes out very well, even though it is not as well known. There is an enormous possibility there of projecting a stronger sense of the antiquity of our culture, of the different strands of it — the Celtic, the Viking, the Norman, the way in which the English and Irish mixing together has enriched our literature, enriched our other forms, our dance, our visual arts, and so on. I believe that there is an opportunity in Europe for Ireland to project its culture, and by doing so to have much more linkages with other countries.

Are you suggesting that to date Ireland has been seen too much in terms of television images of violence or tourist images of fishing and hunting...

To a large extent, I think we are still a hidden country, in particular as far as our culture is concerned. It is not known to many Europeans, many people elsewhere, that we have our own national language, and a culture based on that language. It's not often known abroad how much archaeological and historical wealth we have here in Ireland. A good example was when the President of Iceland, President Vigdis Sinneogadottir, came to visit: she had a background in theatre, and therefore knew a lot about Irish theatre, about Beckett, and writers like Joyce. They had been translated into Icelandic. She was very open and receptive to our culture. She went to Newgrange, she went to Clonmacnois. When she came back to Dublin after these visits, she was full of enthusiasm, and clearly when she went back to Iceland, she spoke about it. I understand that something like four per cent of the population of Iceland has come to Ireland since. A very useful flow of tourists who came basically for two things

— for shopping before Christmas, and for culture. Because their eyes had been opened to Irish culture. I think there is enormous potential for that with other Scandinavian countries, and it's a two-way process. We can learn from their culture too. There is also a very real possibility with the countries of central and eastern Europe, because countries like Romania have a strong Celtic background, as do a number of other countries. Indeed, the Celtic heritage is really the pan-European one. It's the strongest pan-European basic culture, and we in Ireland have a unique role in that Celtic culture.

The examples you cite are drawn mainly from the past, from the area of archaeology and antiquity, but is there not a sense in which that cultural heritage needs to be complemented by more contemporary areas of expression, which would include the electronic media of television, cinema, and popular music, where Ireland has had extraordinary success recently, both nationally and internationally?

Yes, I think those areas represent the kind of creativity that is undoubtedly in Ireland at the moment. Countries go through different cycles, but it has been a very enriching experience for me, to have so many opportunities to see the quality of our artistic expression, be it in the theatre, visual arts, music; and it is evident in what is now being projected in television and cinema to a much wider world, and through pop music. It's also evident in plays like *Dancing at Lughnasa*, expressing a raw inner truth which, like *The Commitments*, draws out of real experience. That is what communicates, that is what gains the wider audience. I have no doubt that our participation in Europe has unleashed and encouraged that sort of creativity in the arts.

Why?

I think it is part of that maturing. We've come out from under the shadow of a cultural Big Brother next door. We have a much broader spectrum in which to reassess Irish culture and reinforce the linkages with other European countries. It's certainly true that young artists, and writers, and musicians are very happy to work in Ireland now. I opened a sculpture factory recently in Cork, in a big warehouse. There was a sense of excitement about large-scale sculpture, about having a place where sculptors could get together. There was a Japanese sculptor there, and she told me she was delighted to be working in Cork, because she had a freedom to work, and I think what she really meant was that there was a creativity there that she found very stimulating. It's my experience going around the country that this is the state of the arts in Ireland — inevitably underfunded in a country like Ireland — but the most important thing, the innate creativity, is there. It is generating a sense of Irishness in the last part of this century which is much more buoyant about itself, more confident, and therefore able to draw on the old in a way that's very relevant to the modern idiom as well.

So the entry into a larger European Community does not necessarily mean that we have to sacrifice our sense of cultural diversity.

On the contrary. I think that Ireland is in a very good position, because of this creativity, to make a significant contribution culturally to Europe. And that's how we should look at it. I think we shouldn't consider ourselves to be out on the margins. Some of the best creativity comes from what might be called the periphery. The Celtic culture is certainly one of the strongest cultures. And I believe there is that sense of confidence about ourselves reflected in the success of U2 and Hothouse Flowers and Sinéad O'Connor, or the success of films like *The Commitments* and *My Left Foot* and *The Field*, and hopefully many others.